**AN
OWNERS
GUIDE**

ALL YOU NEED TO KNOW ABOUT YOUR...

LABRADOR RETRIEVER

Ann Britton

Acknowledgements

The publishers would like to help the following for help with photography:
Ann Britton (Bowstones), Pat Davies (Holmajor), Sharon Rogers (Woodmist),
David Coode (Warringah), Fiona Hilman (Penworlod), Erica Jayes (Sandylands).
Page 11 and 28 © David Tomlinson; Page 44 © istockphoto.com/HannamariaH.

The question of gender

The 'he' pronoun is used throughout this book instead of the
rather impersonal 'it', but no gender bias is intended.

ISBN

978-1-906305-31-4
1-906305-31-5

Printed and bound in China by PWGS.

Contents

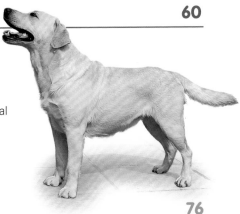

The Essential Labrador Retriever

The eager to please, fun-loving Labrador Retriever, known and loved by so many, is deservedly the most popular breed of dog in the United Kingdom and in the United States of America. He is well known throughout the world for his faithfulness and sterling character. Such is the breed's popularity, that over 45,000 pedigree Labradors are currently bred and registered with the Kennel Club every single year in Britain alone.

This is a breed that enjoys life to the full.

The Labrador's reputation as a tail-wagging friend for life, to old and young alike, has been honed and developed over the last 200 years. He is easy to care for, suffers few ills, and is a most loyal companion, who is faithful to the end of his days – normally, a life spanning 12 to 14 healthy years. I have a happy 16-year old Lab sitting beside me as I write, proving that Labrador ownership is a long-term commitment.

The Labrador is quick to learn and possesses the kindest of natures. He is a multi-purpose dog, easily trained, and hence seen in the role of assistance dog, guide dog, or hearing dog. He performs search and rescue; he is trained to sniff out drugs at ports and airports; in the countryside he is a steady, intelligent, shooting companion, and is an excellent swimmer and retriever.

However, for the majority of Labrador owners, he is their beloved, handsome pet dog and companion, trotting along on a country walk; playing with the family; digging sandcastles on the sea shore; and sharing the sandwiches. On a cold winter's night he will happily cuddle up beside you on the sofa to watch TV, but be aware that he is likely to stretch out over the complete length of the sofa, leaving you with only the floor to sit on! In the summer, he is content to splash about in the paddling pool with the toddlers, or just laze in the shade on the lawn.

The Labrador is wonderful with children and especially gentle with any who are unwell. He understands the human condition and is everyone's trustworthy friend to the end. Quite simply, the Labrador is a dog who will give years of pure devotion.

A Labrador's demands are few. He

needs a regular groom with a stiff brush and comb to keep him clean and tidy; a daily walk or stroll once his puppy days are past; a meal of nourishing food once or twice a day: a comfy bed to lie on in a space free from draughts, and an owner who absolutely adores him.

Labradors love human company – the more, the better. For loyalty, intelligence, ease of care and constant good humour, there is none to equal him.

The Labrador's one fault is his love of his tummy, where a tempting morsel might mysteriously disappear if left within his reach. I recall a whole Christmas cake vanishing when I went to answer the doorbell! But otherwise, he is canine perfection and rightly the choice of millions all over the world.

ORIGINS OF THE LABRADOR

It is intriguing to look back over the centuries, to find out how the breed evolved, for the exact origins are far from clear.

Some 200 years ago, around 1800, the Labrador's ancestors came to Britain from Newfoundland Island, which is situated just south of Labrador on the rugged east coast of Canada.

Evidence suggests that in 1000AD, Viking explorers sailed to mainland Labrador and to Newfoundland Island. Later centuries saw the island occupied by Beothuck Indians. However, there

The Lesser Newfoundland or St John's Dog was generally black in colour.

The outstanding qualities of the Labrador have been prized throughout its history.

was no record of any resident dogs in the area during these times.

In the 15th and 16th centuries, in Europe, more than 2,000 miles away on the other side of the Atlantic Ocean, dogs similar to present-day Labradors were depicted in splendid Spanish, Italian and Portuguese oil paintings, often standing next to, or lying at the foot of, the subject of the painting, a person of noble birth.

The 16th century was a time when European explorers travelled the world by sea, and traders regularly sailed back and forth between continents. Fishing fleets crossed the Atlantic Ocean to trawl the rich cod banks off Newfoundland. On board ship,

included as part of the working crew, were their working dogs. Did these dogs perhaps resemble the dogs from the noble European paintings and were they the forerunners of the Labrador?

Newfoundland Island is surrounded by seawater, chilled by the Labrador Current, which flows south from the Arctic Circle. Fishing in the cod-filled waters of the Grand Banks proved so plentiful that eventually, over the years, fishermen from England, and later Portugal and Spain, settled for good at St Johns in the south-east of Newfoundland. Of course, the working dogs, which had accompanied them across the ocean, stayed too.

TWO TYPES EMERGE

Over time, the settlers' dogs bred with local dogs. Probably these had also arrived in Newfoundland via ships from various parts of the world.

Two distinct types of dog evolved in the area, and 19th century writers talk of the Newfoundland Dog (similar to today's Newfoundland) and the Lesser Newfoundland Dog, also known as the St John's Dog, ancestor of the Labrador.

In the early 1800s, a renowned wildfowler, Colonel Peter Hawker, an Englishman, who was one of the foremost shooting sportsmen of the time, owned a trading schooner, which sailed back and forth across the Atlantic Ocean between Poole, on the south coast of England, and Newfoundland Island. He observed and wrote about the two types of dog, which inhabited Newfoundland.

In 1814 in his book, *Instructions to Young Sportsmen*, he described the Newfoundland Dog as: "a very large dog, strong of limb, with rough hair and carrying his tail high." These dogs were the ancestors of today's Newfoundlands. The other type of dog, the Lesser Newfoundland Dog or St John's Dog, the forebear of our Labradors, Colonel Hawker described as:

"...by far the best for any kind of shooting dog. He is generally black and no bigger than a Pointer, very fine in legs, with short, smooth hair and does not carry his tail so much curled as the other, (Newfoundland); he is extremely quick, running, swimming... his sense of smell is hardly to be credited. In finding wounded game there is not a living equal in the canine race. He is chiefly used on the native coast by fishermen...."

THE PERFECT WORKING RETRIEVER

The St John's Dog's short, thick waterproof coat, which repelled ice, (unlike his larger, hairier cousin, the Newfoundland), his swimming ability, coupled with his strength, trainability and utter enthusiasm for life meant that the dogs were excellent workers and an important part of the fishing trade.

Being tough, hardy and medium-sized, they happily toiled alongside the fishermen, in the chilly climate.

Swimming in the freezing cold waters, they retrieved cod that had escaped from the fishing hooks or nets. They rescued crewmembers who had fallen overboard and they fetched objects that had slipped into the water. They hauled in the fishing nets, and, at the end of the day, towed the fishing boats ashore, up the shelved beaches, to be moored safely for the night.

There are tales of foggy days when, to avoid collision, a St John's

The early pioneers were filled with enthusiasm for the breed's working ability.

Dog sitting beside a fisherman in his boat, would bark to alert others of their location; stories tell of dogs swimming considerable distances from one boat to another, carrying messages. On land they were even used to haul wood on sledges from inaccessible places. The wood was then stacked and later used to smoke fish. It appears the St John's Dog could turn his paw to any job required!

Newfoundland was also home to a plentiful source of game birds. The settlers found the St John's Dogs were ideal hunting companions, easily retrieving the shot game.

Such was the dogs' energy, their eager to please nature and enthusiasm for life that having finished one job, they were always ready and waiting for the next. By the end of the day, still in excellent humour, they were quite content to settle down to relax and amuse the family's children.

I know many of you who own Labradors today will recognise so many of these endearing characteristics, including their love of water, of retrieving and delight in human companionship – all inherited directly from the St John's Dogs.

COMING TO BRITAIN

In the early 1800s, trading ships returning from Newfoundland to England carried St John's Dogs back to Poole in Dorset. Such was their reputation as sportsmen's dogs, being excellent swimmers and retrievers, they were quickly acquired by the

There are tales of the first St John's dogs swimming ashore when they first arrived in England.

sporting aristocracy. It is probable that similar St John's Dogs were also landed at other ports around Britain, including Greenock in Scotland.

The 2nd Earl of Malmesbury of Heron Court, near Poole in Dorset, acquired St John's Dogs from trading ships returning to Poole harbour, and he established his kennel in the early years of the 19th century. Unlike the Wavy Coat Retrievers and the Golden Retrievers, which had been produced by crossbreeding, his kennel was solely based on the pure St John's Dogs.

His son, the 3rd Earl of Malmesbury, born in 1807, also imported and bred purely from the St John's Dogs, never crossing with other breeds. He called the dogs he bred Labradors.

Just as had been seen in Newfoundland, the 3rd Earl recognised his Labradors' great potential as highly accomplished retrievers. They had a particular type and character of their own, which he wanted to preserve: working over the wet and marshy duck-shooting grounds of his estates, his dogs proved their worth. Soon he built up a breeding kennel based solely on the St John's Dogs, which were landed at Poole, and, luckily for historians of the breed, he maintained precise breeding records from the very outset.

Colonel Peter Hawker, who had observed the St John's Dogs in Newfoundland so many years before, continued to import them for the Earl of Malmesbury's breeding programme until 1875.

THE SCOTTISH LINK

While, in the south of England, the 2nd and 3rd Earls of Malmesbury were breeding from their St Johns' Dogs, in the Scottish Borders, keen sportsmen – the 5th Duke of Buccleuch, born 1806, and his brother, Lord John Scott, born 1809, plus the Earls of Home and their families – had also been importing and breeding pure St John's Dogs.

Nell pictured in 1867. Note the white muzzle and white feet.

These Scottish, Victorian aristocrats certainly enjoyed the companionship of their Labradors, just as we do now. In 1839, many years before the Quarantine Act was introduced to prevent the spread of rabies from mainland Europe to Britain, the 5th Duke of Buccleuch sailed on his yacht to Naples with his black Labrador, Moss, accompanied by the 10th Earl of Home and his black Labrador, Drake.

One of the early photographs of a Labrador is of the 11th Earl of Home's black bitch, Nell, taken in 1867 when she was 12 years of age. It shows a typical Labrador of the time, used for shooting in England and Scotland. She was black-coated with a pure white muzzle and four pure white feet, and, apart from the white, looking not so very different to our present-day black Labradors.

COMMON ANCESTORS

In Victorian Britain, some of the early imported St John's Dogs had been crossed with English Setters, which were already well established as an English sporting breed. The offspring were called Wavy Coated Retrievers and these generally black dogs were the most popular shooting dogs of the mid-Victorian times. The Wavy Coated Retriever was the ancestor of today's Flat Coated Retrievers.

Occasionally, gold or liver-coloured Wavy Coated Retrievers were born. In 1868 Lord Tweedmouth of Guisachan in Scotland crossed one of his gold Wavy Coated Retrievers with a gold Tweed Spaniel. The progeny of this double gold mating were all golden in colour and were the first Golden Retrievers.

The first Labradors were pure St John's Dogs crossed with pure St John's Dogs. The Labrador is cousin to the Flat Coated Retriever and second cousin to the Golden Retriever; all breeds initially stemming from the St John's Dogs.

FORGING A LINK

In the early 1880s, the 6th Duke of Buccleuch and the 12th Earl of Home were visiting Bournemouth during the winter and joined a shooting party on the Malmesbury estate. Observing the Earl of Malmesbury's dogs, they were amazed at the way they worked, especially in water. These dogs, although based on the same pure St John's Dogs as their own Scottish dogs, were in a totally different category. The Earl of Malmesbury made a gift of three of his homebred Labradors to the Scottish Buccleuch kennels: Ned (born in 1882) and Avon (born 1885) and Nell (birthdate unknown), and this established a strong link between the two kennels.

In 1887 the Earl of Malmesbury wrote to the 6th Duke of Buccleuch: "I always call my dogs Labradors. The breed may be known by having a close coat which turns off water like oil and a thick otter tail". They were described as: "Small, compact and very active; their coats short, thick and smooth with sometimes a brown tinge at certain seasons. The eyes of most are something like burnt sugar in colour. Their heads, which are not big, are broad and the skull shapely and not long in muzzle. Their bright countenances denote their sweet tempers and high courage."

With great enthusiasm, a joint breeding programme was established between the Scottish Buccleuch and Home kennels, and the English kennel of the Earl of Malmesbury. When the bloodlines were combined, an excellent Labrador Retriever strain developed with a consistency in type from one generation to the next.

From 1882, all breeding records were noted down and these formed the first Labrador studbook.

In 1888, Lord George Scott, younger son of the 6th Duke of Buccleuch, took over the management of the Buccleuch Labradors in Scotland. At that time there were more than 60 gamekeepers on 450,000 acres of the various Buccleuch estates. Within a few years, every Buccleuch gamekeeper was provided with one or more purebred Labradors. Such was Lord George Scott's enthusiasm for the breed that he planned all the matings and oversaw the rearing of all the puppies, so that the correct type of Labrador, to which he and his family and friends had devoted so much time and effort, was maintained.

The establishment of good bloodlines in Britain proved essential, as, by 1885, imports of dogs to England from Newfoundland had subsided and eventually the trade ceased. Newfoundland became a sheep farming area and the

The three Labrador colours – yellow, black and chocolate – have existed from the early days of the breed's development.

Newfoundland Sheep Protection Act was in force. Keeping dogs was discouraged. Many dogs were destroyed and heavy taxes were imposed on dog owners. Residents of Newfoundland were allowed to keep only one dog per family. Bitches were taxed higher than dogs, and most bitch puppies were therefore destroyed at birth.

In 1895 the Quarantine Act 1895 was introduced to Britain in a bid to stop the spread of rabies. This brought about the end of imports of St John's Dogs from Newfoundland. Sadly, by the middle of the 20th century, in its homeland of Newfoundland, the St John's Dogs became extinct.

However, the Labrador's future in Britain was assured thanks to the dedication of the Earls of Malmesbury, Home and the Dukes of Buccleugh and their families and friends. The Labrador's reputation as a retriever was already beginning to outstrip that of the highly regarded, black Wavy Coated Retriever.

COAT COLOURS

The three colours – black, yellow and chocolate (originally called liver) – have always existed from the early days of the 19th century dog from Newfoundland Island. It is probable that the imported St John's Dogs carried the gene for all three colours. However, the Victorian breeders in England and Scotland generally selected for the black coat colour, culling the majority of pups of other colours.

The fashion for black was mirrored in other retrieving breeds, which stemmed from the St John's Dogs, too. The Wavy Coat/Flat Coated Retrievers, which were a cross between the St John's Dog and English Setters, also produced the three colours within a litter and occasionally still do today. Breeders tended to select for black.

In 1892 the birth of the first liver puppies was recorded. Although colours other than black had appeared in litters prior to this date, liver and yellow puppies were not in demand and went un-noted and were often culled. The first two recorded liver puppies were sired by Buccleugh Avon, who was one of the three dogs initially given by the Earl of Malmesbury to the Duke of Buccleugh. Thus, Buccleugh Avon is probably behind many of today's popular chocolate Labradors.

In 1899 the first recorded yellow, Ben of Hyde, was born in a litter of black puppies from two black parents at Major Radcliff's kennel. This dog was the foundation of the early yellow Labrador kennels.

BREED RECOGNITION

The Kennel Club, an organisation to oversee the registration of pedigree dogs and to run licensed dog shows, was established in 1873. In 1880 the committee introduced a system of universal registration. The first Retrievers to appear in the Kennel Club Stud Books were all listed together under one general Retriever section, with no separation between any of the different breeds. Therefore, it was possible to register half the pups from a litter as Golden Retrievers and the other half as Labradors! In 1903 the Kennel Club finally listed the Labrador Retriever as a separate breed.

Early records show that in 1912 there were 281 Labradors registered with the Kennel Club; 10 years later that figure had risen to 916. In 2009, over 45,000 were KC registered. In North America, the Labrador has topped registrations of all breeds since 1991 up to the present day.

THE LABRADOR RETRIEVER CLUB

In 1916, the Labrador Retriever Club was founded. The committee members were responsible for setting up the guidelines for the breed's development. The objectives of the club were to encourage the breeding of pure, sound Labradors; to protect the type of Labrador that had proved itself so eminently suitable for work; to encourage field trials and shows, and to ensure that qualified judges officiated at both. A Breed Standard was drawn up to ensure breeders maintained the correct Labrador type.

Naming The Breed

No one really knows for certain how the Labrador Retriever got its name. Obviously, the Retriever part is clear. In the early days, it was a fish or a shot game-bird that was retrieved; today, it is more likely to be a tennis ball, a plastic plant pot, the TV remote control, or your spectacle case – but Labradors have always loved to retrieve things!

How the name Labrador came about may be quite accidental. Was it a simple geographical mistake? Perhaps the English aristocrats who imported the first St John's Dogs were uncertain of the precise geographical location of the island of Newfoundland and mistakenly thought it was part of neighbouring Labrador. Hence, they called the dogs that hailed from that vicinity, Labradors.

Another suggestion is that early pictures of the Portuguese workers' dog, Cane di Castro Laboreiro, show a very marked similarity to the Labrador.

Did Portuguese sailors arrive in Newfoundland bringing with them their Laboreiro, and did these dogs cross with those of the English settlers? Did the title Labrador come from the name Laboreiro the labourer? We will never know.

The first chairman of the Labrador Club was the Hon. Arthur Holland Hibbert (later Lord Knutsford), a keen, dedicated Labrador breeder. He had started his Munden kennel in 1894, based on a bitch, Munden Sybil, whose ancestors came direct from Newfoundland. His bitch, Munden Single, born in March 1899, was the first Labrador to run in a field trial in 1904, winning a Certificate of Merit at the International Gundog League's stake at Sherbourne. In an article in *Our Dogs* 1904 she was referred to as the "finest Labrador bitch ever seen on or off the bench."

The secretary of the newly formed Labrador Retriever Club was Mrs Quintin-Dick (later, Lorna, Countess Howe). She spared no effort in promoting the breed to which she was devoted. Her name and that of her Banchory kennel are famous to this day throughout the Labrador world. Banchory dogs won every possible honour, both as superb gundogs at field trials and also in the show ring.

THE GREAT BOLO

Ch. Banchory Bolo, born in 1915, was probably Countess Howe's most famous dog; he is behind most of today's Labradors of all colours. The famous white hairs under his feet, fondly described as Bolo pads, still appear on some blacks to this very day. Judges who are unaware of this historical link to one of our breed's great forefathers sometimes regard 'Bolo pads' as a fault; others regard them with affection – a gentle reminder and link to founding years past.

Bolo was the first Dual Champion Labrador – a Champion in both the show ring and at field trials – and so important in the history of the breed.

THE YELLOW LABRADOR RETRIEVER CLUB

In 1923, eight years after the Labrador Retriever Club was established, it became clear that there was a need for a breed club to specifically promote the interests of the yellow Labradors and thus the Yellow Labrador Club was formed that year. Major Radcliffe (Zelstone) was chairman, Lord Lonsdale was

Dual Ch. Banchory Bob: A fine representative of the Banchory kennel who won his dual Championship in the field and in the show ring.

president, and Mr Montgomery Parker was secretary.

The reason why a specific colour-related club was required followed an incident at a dog show during 1923. A steward tried to exclude a yellow Labrador dog from a Labrador class at a show, because he believed that it could not possibly be a Labrador as it was not black!

The dog's owner, another renowned, stalwart character of the breed's history, Mrs Veronica Wormald, owner of the Knaith kennel, insisted that she would most certainly show her yellow dog in the class, as he was without doubt a Labrador. He went on to win a prize in the class, but the incident highlighted the need for a specific club to promote the interests of the yellow Labrador. The club flourishes to this very day, holding field trials and two shows annually, a Championship show for all three colours, and an Open show specifically reserved for yellow Labradors.

WHAT SHOULD A LABRADOR LOOK LIKE?

When the first Labrador Retriever breed club was founded in 1916, the committee drew up an ideal blueprint for the breed. This was called the

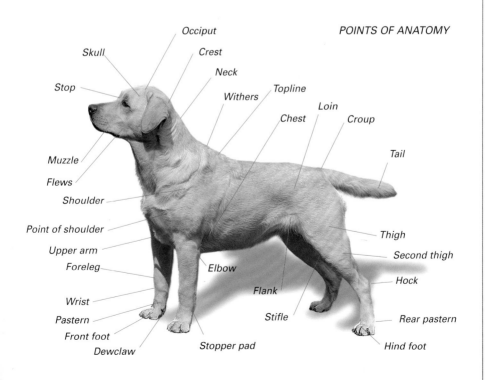

POINTS OF ANATOMY

Occiput
Skull
Crest
Neck
Stop
Withers
Topline
Loin
Chest
Croup
Muzzle
Flews
Tail
Shoulder
Point of shoulder
Thigh
Upper arm
Second thigh
Foreleg
Elbow
Hock
Flank
Wrist
Stifle
Pastern
Rear pastern
Front foot
Stopper pad
Hind foot
Dewclaw

Breed Standard and was a written description of what a well-bred Labrador should look like and to differentiate it from any other breed.

Labrador breeders have, since that time, aimed to maintain the character and looks of the Labradors they breed according to the Breed Standard, which has changed very little over the years. In 2009 a clause to encourage owners to watch their Labradors' waistlines was introduced, but otherwise little of the wording has been changed since the early days.

Despite having just one Labrador Breed Standard, which should apply to all Labradors, over the years differences have crept in between the show Labrador on the one hand and the field trial or working Labrador on the other. The show Labrador breeders aim to maintain the Breed Standard looks and characteristics against which the dog is judged in the show ring. However, some owners of working Labradors and field trial dogs are more interested in the dog's working ability and speed rather than its precise looks. Thus sadly, over time the working Labrador's appearance has strayed from the Breed Standard. The dogs tend to be taller, finer built, with finer bone, untypical heads and a busy temperament, which can make them less appealing as family pets than the more easygoing show-bred dogs.

THE BREED STANDARD

All pedigree breeds of dog have their own individual Kennel Club Breed Standard, which clearly differentiates one particular breed from any other. The Labrador should closely resemble the Labrador Breed Standard, and in so doing there will be no question that he really is a Labrador.

General appearance

The Standard ensures the Labrador is built to perform his task as a gundog for long hours, picking up and carrying heavy game without strain. His intelligent, kind temperament and ease of training make him popular. He should be a strongly built, well balanced, short coupled, active dog; a sturdy animal with substance and energy.

Head and skull

His skull is broad with a definite stop. The 'stop' is almost a right angle between his brow and his muzzle.

The length of the skull from the occiput (the slightly raised point at the centre-back of the skull) to the stop is similar to the length of the muzzle, which should be broad and level, not snipey, when viewed from the top and the side. The nostrils should be wide.

The eyes are set square in the skull, neither slanted upwards nor downwards; they are brown, the colour of burnt sugar, almond shaped, never round or bulbous; their melting expression reflecting kindness and intelligence.

The cheek, below the eye, should be chiseled, not full.

The ears, soft as velvet, are set well back. Ideally, if held across the eye on the same side, the ear should just reach the inner corner of that eye.

without falling off.

The neck is of medium length, being longer on top than underneath. The throat is clean, with no excess hanging skin, known as throatiness.

There should be no rucks or unsightly rolls across his shoulder, pointing to either imperfect front construction, or excess weight and lack of coat.

Dentition

A 'scissor bite' is required, with the top teeth closely overlapping the bottom teeth. He should have 42 strong, white teeth. Occasionally, some premolars are missing.

Conformation

The outline should be clean in profile; broad with plenty of heart room when viewed from the front; strong and muscular when viewed from the rear.

Neck

The neck-line should flow into his level top-line with no sharp angles. The quarters should not fall away at the croup.

An imaginary marble, placed at the top of the neck, should roll slowly down the neck across the shoulder, level topline and quarters to the tail,

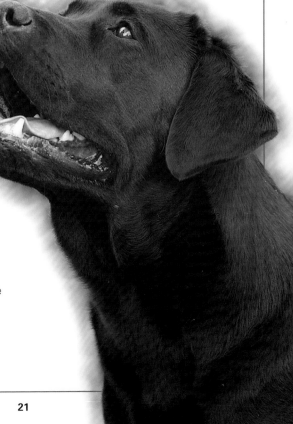

The Labrador has a broad skull, with ears set well back, and eyes the colour of burnt sugar.

If front construction is correct, the overall conformation is likely to be correct.

Front construction

If this is correct, the Labrador can perform his task as a gundog with ease; if it is wrong, he will constantly jar himself, having no springing to cushion his movement.

Look for the front construction triangle, which holds the secret. If the front is made right, the rest will normally follow.

The first side of the triangle is a vertical line dropped from the shoulder at the withers (where the top of the neckline meets the back). This vertical line should pass through the back of the elbow. If the line falls well behind the elbow, even though the dog's shoulder blade may be of the correct length and angle, the upper arm will be too short and upright.

The second side of the triangle is the shoulder blade. Of good length it leaves the withers, slopes down to the point of shoulder at the front of the chest, where it makes a 90-degree angle with the upper arm. If it is too short, the dog will have difficulty picking up heavy objects.

The third side of the triangle is the upper arm, between the elbow joint and the point of shoulder. This bone is often incorrectly too short in length and instead of being angled forward, is almost upright, which gives the dog no 'springing' when moving, just a horrible jarring.

If a Labrador has short upper arm construction he will not move in the required easy, energy-saving strides. Instead, he will move with tiring, short, rapid 'dolly steps'. The upper arm should be at an angle of 145 degrees to the vertical foreleg at the elbow; the angle of a policeman's arm held high, having instructed you to halt!

Forelegs

From the side, leg length should

reflect a proportion of 50/50 withers to elbow, elbow to ground. Well-boned forelegs are strong and straight. Excessive bone is incorrect, as is weak spindly bone.

Pasterns are strong with slight flexibility. The bone below the pastern should be the same as that above the pastern, not tapering.

The feet should face forward, not turning out or in, with neat, well-arched toes and well-developed pads. Long, flat toes, splayed or open feet are all incorrect.

Body

The ribcage is wide, well sprung and barrel shaped, of good length, especially in breeding bitches. The ribs leave the spine almost horizontally compared to other breeds. Slab sides, where the rib cage is flat, are incorrect, as are short ribcages where there is little length from front to back. The topline should be level with no dipping behind the shoulder.

The chest is deep and wide, the brisket between the forelegs coming

The Labrador is short-coupled with a deep wide chest.

The essential Labrador combining the conformation and character which makes the breed unique.

down at least to the level of the elbow.

The Labrador is short-coupled, to ensure the loin, the area between the back of the ribs and the quarters, is strong. He should be neither too fat nor too thin, but well covered with some sign of a waist.

Hindquarters

Viewed from above, the quarters are wider than the front assembly. They are broad and strong, not falling away at the croup; the tail comes straight off the back.

From the rear, the quarters should be wide, strong and well muscled.

In profile, the well-developed second thighs should resemble the shape of a generous ham. There should be a good bend of stifle but not an over-angulated stifle, which sets the leg too far back, causing weakness.

The hocks should be well let down and perpendicular to the ground, neither sloping in under the body (sickle hocks) nor set excessively far back.

Movement

Correct construction produces

straight, true, driving movement with unexaggerated, ground-covering, easy-flowing strides.

Front movement faults

The forelegs should come straight forwards, neither pinning in, towards each other, caused by being 'out at elbow', nor with outwardly flapping feet from being 'tied at elbow'.

Hind movement faults

Hind movement should be square, converging slightly with pace. Faulty construction includes: too wide behind; cow-hocks, which produce a sideways thrust rather than forwards impulsion; rubbing hocks, which are so close together they almost brush; crossing hind feet.

Tail

The otter tail is well covered with coat, without feathering, and is used for balance when swimming. It reaches to the hock and is wide at the root gradually tapering to a point.

Coat and colours

The waterproof coat of the Labrador is a short-length, double coat; a harsh top-coat overlying a dense soft woolly undercoat; never open textured. The recognised colours are whole-coloured black, yellow and chocolate.

Breed Essentials

The Labrador must look like a Labrador and no other breed of dog. Above all, the Labrador 'must haves' are:

- A kind temperament
- A beautifully chiselled shape to his broad head and muzzle
- A soft, gentle expression with warm, brown, burnt-sugar coloured eyes
- A double coat, harsh on top with woolly undercoat, often nearly grey underneath on black dogs
- An otter tail.

Breeders of every breed of dog strive to attain perfection according to their Breed Standard, but Mother Nature is usually one step ahead of us.

The perfect dog, who fulfils every single requirement of its Breed Standard, has yet to be born, which is why dog breeding is so intriguing and continues to be such an absorbing hobby.

Choosing A Labrador

Before you buy your Labrador puppy be sure that everyone in the household really wants a dog. As a parent, do not buy a Labrador purely because your children have fallen for a cuddly 'Andrex puppy'. This stage is quickly over as the puppy grows larger month by month. Your children may well promise to care for their Labrador forever, before and after school, and many will do so. But once the novelty has worn off, the task often falls to Mum or Dad. So, only buy a Labrador if you think it is a brilliant idea, have the time to spare, and really want one yourself.

POINTS TO CONSIDER

A Labrador lives between 12 and 14 years. Do you have room in your life and your home for this lifelong commitment? When he is young, he will want activity; in his later years, he will want a gentle stroll and a warm, comfy bed to snooze in.

Have you considered the weekly cost of feeding and caring for your Labrador, including possible vet bills or insurance premiums?

Labradors get lonely and can get into mischief if left alone for hours on end. Is there someone at home or who can visit him during the day? Have you a well-fenced garden? It must be at least 5 ft (1.5 m) high. Where will you exercise the adult dog each day and who will do the walking?

What about foreign holidays? Are there boarding kennels nearby, or will you take your dog abroad with you or stay in the UK?

PERFECT PARTNERS

Labradors thrive on human company. It is not kind to take one on and then leave him at home on his own all day long with no company. In fact, if everyone is out at work from 9am till 5pm, it would be better to forget the dog-owning idea for a while and wait until circumstances change before proceeding.

An ideal Labrador owner is someone who has time to spend with their dog each day; someone who is at home; an owner who can enjoy every minute of Labrador companionship and devotion. Of course, this ideal is rarely possible these days and Labradors find

Bear in mind, a cuddly eight-week-old puppy will become a lively, energetic adult with an ever-wagging tail and a bottomless stomach.

excellent homes with those who manage to be at home at some time during the day. It could be someone who works mornings only, or is able to come back at lunchtime to go for a 30-minute walk. Some owners work from home and some people are able to take the dog to work, as long as he does not have to be left in the car for any length of time.

The main requirement is that a Labrador should never be abandoned all day long. He needs human contact, mental stimulation and exercise.

LABRADOR CHARACTERISTICS

When contemplating taking on a cuddly eight-week-old Labrador puppy, you should be aware that Labrador puppies quickly grow into lively medium-sized dogs, 21.5-22.5 ins (54-57 cms) high at the withers (where the neck meets the back), and eventually weighing from 63-77 lbs (28-35 kgs). They live, on average, 12 to 14 years and have few health problems. Labradors are happy, healthy, companionable dogs, who love human company (and food); they are intelligent, placid, easily trained and easy to care for, with a fun-loving, loyal temperament, which is why they are so extremely popular around the world.

Their main weaknesses as pets come from their innocent, friendly enthusiasm and joy for life. The ever-wagging tail can easily sweep the contents of a coffee table on to the

Working Labradors are bred purely for their ability to perform in the field, and they do not conform to the stipulations of the Breed Standard.

floor; their love of water and splashing around among the water lilies in the ornamental fish-pond can be unappreciated.

Labradors adore retrieving, and this is not confined to toys; books, papers, the TV remote, abandoned shoes, and the contents of the laundry bin, all may, at some time, be found neatly collected together in your Labrador's bed, hopefully not chewed

One thing, which has to be watched throughout a Labrador's life is his waistline. A Labrador has a passion for food and an ability to melt your heart with one imploring look. He will easily convince you that he is suffering extreme hunger and needs just one more treat. Unfortunately, where food is concerned, Labradors are morally challenged; their self-service instinct is extremely well developed. Therefore, food must be kept out of reach and additional treats kept to a minimum.

A Labrador puppy is full of mischief, but you will have lots of fun watching him grow up.

FINDING A LABRADOR

Over a lifetime, it costs less to feed and house a well-bred, healthy Labrador from health-checked parents for up to 14 years, than to care for a poor, sickly example, who hardly resembles the breed, has no papers, no health checks, and requires frequent and expensive veterinary attention throughout his life. So where do you go to find a typical, healthy Labrador?

It is a good idea to visit the Kennel Club Discover Dogs event, which is held each year at Earls Court, London and at Crufts in the National Exhibition Centre, Birmingham. Here you will meet Labrador breed club representatives happy to show you their Labradors and discuss the joys and pitfalls of the breed as pets.

Remember, while a Pug dog looks like a Pug dog and nothing else, in just the same way the Labrador, if purebred, conforms to the Labrador Breed Standard and resembles no other breed of dog.

Show-bred or working?

In both the UK and the USA, a divergence has gradually occurred between Labradors bred for conformation classes in the show ring and thus fitting the Breed Standard, and those bred purely for their working ability in the shooting field, who come in all shapes and sizes.

In my opinion, the laidback show-bred Labrador makes the perfect pet. Some working-bred Labradors settle down well as pets too, but others can be very busy animals who would rather live outside in a kennel, performing the working task their ancestors were initially bred for, rather than sitting quietly, in comfort, by the fireside.

Puppy or adult?

In most cases, people opt for buying a puppy, but there are points worthy of consideration, and it may suit your lifestyle to take on an older dog or a rescued dog that needs rehoming.

Eight-week-old puppy: The rewarding, yet full-time job of rearing a young puppy, somewhat akin to a human toddler, requires much care and patience. Labrador puppies are bundles of adorable fun and bring much joy and laughter from their antics as they grow and mature and gradually turn your home into their haven. If you take on a puppy, you have to be one step ahead of him at all times.

In later years, you will recall fond memories of his antics during his first months with you: his escapades in the garden pruning the plants; the trimmed curtains; the chewed plaster; the day he fell in the pond; the clean washing he pulled from the line and dragged around the muddy lawn; the eaten TV control, or, once in a lifetime – yes, it's true – the swallowed still-wriggling frog!

All naughty at the time, but so amusing once he has become a superbly mannered sober adult and the memories are viewed through rose-tinted spectacles.

Puppies can go to their new homes from eight weeks of age. At this age, a pup is immature and playful, and has much growing and sleeping to do. He is like a blank canvas; he knows nothing and it is up to you to teach him everything he needs to learn to grow into a

If you choose an older pup, you will be able to judge his temperament, and you will have a better idea how he will look as an adult.

well-adjusted adult.

A young puppy has a little stomach and needs regular small meals four times daily: breakfast, lunch, tea and supper. He will not be house trained, and for many months he will not be ready for serious exercise. Teething occurs when a puppy is around four months of age, and during this time your puppy's gums will be sore and he will be more inclined to chew.

An older pup (6-8 months):
Sometimes there is an opportunity to buy a slightly older, 'pick of the litter' puppy, a special pup, run on to show by the breeder. Perhaps the pup has not made the grade for the show ring for some minor cosmetic reason; maybe he carries his tail too high, or too low; perhaps his ears are on the large side. This is a wonderful chance to buy a really top-class puppy, one who would never have been available

to purchase as a pet from a show kennel at eight weeks of age.

Plus points of the older puppy:

- His good temperament will be obvious.
- He will need only two meals per day compared with four meals required by a baby puppy.
- His inoculations will be complete and any complications or reactions to these will have been dealt with.
- Puppyhood illnesses or defects are extremely rare, but any there might have been would have been obvious by three months and well cleared up by six months.
- He will have been house trained, lead trained, and socialised with other dogs, children and people.
- Puppies in this 'six-month onwards' age group can start going for short walks, whereas baby puppies cannot.
- The puppy's baby teeth will have been shed from 16 weeks of age. By six months his adult teeth will be through and chewing to ease his sore gums will have decreased.
- At six months of age you will get a good idea of how your Labrador will look in adulthood.

The adult Labrador: Older Labradors will suit those who do not want the trouble of rearing and training a young puppy, but who want a well-behaved, trusty Labrador to love and to take out

from day one. Occasionally, show kennels have older dogs available; perhaps they have not made the grade in the show ring or they just do not take to the show ring, are bored with it, and give the clear impression they would rather be enjoying the outdoors, swimming in the pond or walking in the hills.

These older Labradors, past their puppy and adolescent stages, are always in demand. Being fully trained and fully grown, the breeding, type and temperament will be there for you to clearly see. He will fit in immediately with your family, and his pedigree will prove he comes from the best of health-checked parents.

An adult Labrador makes a wonderful fit and healthy pet who, from the start, will march happily beside you and your family all day long, and enjoy sharing the lunchtime picnic. He will settle in well, aided by the fact that a Labrador adores the wonderful person who last fed him. A walk, a full tummy and a warm companionable fireside… heaven! What more could a dog desire?

The rescued Labrador

There are several excellent registered Labrador rescue charities from which you can obtain a Labrador. The rescue organisations are often allied to the Labrador breed clubs situated around the country. Their addresses are available from the Kennel Club.

The rescue centres individually rehome thousands of unwanted Labradors every year in the UK. There are Labradors of all ages in rescue. Some arrive at the rescue's door through sad circumstances, such as the divorce or death of their owners. Other dogs come from owners who, for one reason or another, should probably never have taken on a Labrador in the first place. At some point they decide they do not want their Labrador any more, often for the flimsiest of reasons. "Oh, we're going on holiday", or "It's Christmas, we're having a new settee!"

It is a sad predicament, but at least the rescued dog faces a much better life of love and comfort once he is rehomed.

If you apply for a rescued dog, be prepared for your home and lifestyle to be thoroughly vetted by the rescue organisers. This is not an insult but has to be done to ensure that the home is permanent, suitable and that, once rehomed, these formerly unfortunate dogs will

It can be very rewarding to give a rescued dog a second chance.

Puppies of the same colour seem to seek each other out.

live a long, happy, fulfilled life with you and never suffer upheaval again.

COLOUR CHOICES

Labradors come in three different whole colours: black, chocolate and yellow. No other colours are recognised.

There is often surprise when visitors see a Labrador litter containing all three colours; puppies lying in the nest whose coats are perfect, whole-coloured black, chocolate or yellow. People generally think that a litter would be all of the same whole-coloured puppies, i.e. all black pups or all yellow or all chocolate, but no, if both parents carry the genes for the three colours, then in all probability there will be representatives of each perfect colour within the litter.

The only times when all the puppies in a litter are the same colour are either when both parents are yellow themselves (in which case all the puppies are yellow), or if one of the parents is dominant black, in which case all the puppies are black. Other than these exceptions, there is often the chance of black, chocolate and yellow puppies appearing in a litter.

Observing a mixed colour litter of Labrador puppies you will also see that the separate colours often seek each other out right from birth, well before their eyes have opened at around 14 days. They will often lie in the whelping bed arranged in groups of each different colour: black with black, yellow with yellow, and chocolate with chocolate. What instinct causes this is unknown, perhaps the coat colours smell differently to the immature, as yet unsighted pups, but it is quite amazing to see them snuggled in their little colour-coded groups.

Black

This is the traditional Labrador colour, so popular and successful in the show ring, the shooting field, and as wonderful, faithful pets. The black coat is double – harsh on top with a woolly undercoat, which is often mouse-grey in colour. A single, shiny black coat with no woolly undercoat is incorrect. The coat is to keep the dog warm and dry.

To those who have never considered a black Labrador, I always say that if you can appreciate a diamond and see into its multi-coloured beauty, then you can easily learn to "see" and understand the beauties of a black Labrador. While the yellow Labrador is instantly appealing because of its warm colour, you really have to look into the blacks and know exactly what you are looking at to see their qualities.

Initially, you might think of a black dog as just a black blob, all the same colour all over. Look again, and gradually you will see much more: the different directions of the hair growth on the body; the lights and shades of blackness defining the head shape and highlighting his beautiful brown eyes. Bit by bit you will see so much more than the initial black blob! Beware, once you have fallen for a black Labrador, I doubt you will ever change your mind or accept another colour.

Black Labradors are quick to learn and I find them most intelligent. They moult twice a year, in spring and in the autumn. In addition to this,

Black: The traditional Labrador colour.

Chocolate: A popular colour, but Labradors of this colour seldom win top honours in the show ring.

bitches usually moult 19 weeks after their season, whether mated or not. Once moulting starts, it will be three months before the coat is fully returned.

Chocolate

Although the first chocolate Labradors were registered in 1892, the colour was not popular. Up to the 1980s just a handful of caring breeders specialised in the chocolate colour. The numbers bred annually were tiny. However, during the 1980s, the appearance of a handsome pair of "rare" chocolate Labradors in a well-known glossy country magazine advert, for green Wellington boots, brought the colour to the fore. Since then, chocolate Labradors have been in great demand as pets, bizarrely often commanding a higher price for their initial rarity, than excellent, top-quality animals of the other coat colours.

Sadly, because of this price excess, in recent years inhumane puppy farms have concentrated on breeding chocolate Labradors *en masse*, more than likely from parents who have not been health checked, and often in horrific conditions, purely to supply a ready pet market, willing to pay an excess for the chocolate colour.

Luckily, there are now many excellent show kennels which produce top-class chocolate Labradors. The chocolate Labrador is no longer a rarity commanding a higher price, which might be its saving. Hopefully in future, the selective commercial breeding of chocolate Labradors will prove less lucrative to puppy farmers, although, sadly, as long as people foolishly buy puppies from these sources, I doubt the trade will ever cease completely.

When looking at an adult, chocolate Labrador, ideally they should have an even-coloured dark brown double coat, dark brown pigment, and brown eyes. Their eyes should certainly not be yellow or green, as I have seen on more than one occasion. Chocolates make good pets, are sometimes trained to the gun and used in the field (although some say they are harder to train than blacks). In the show ring, they have an uphill struggle to win at top level, not everyone appreciating the colour, however they are exhibited, some with considerable success. A really good chocolate Labrador in the show ring is a joy to behold.

Chocolate Labradors moult the same as black Labradors – twice yearly – and bitches normally 19 weeks after their season, whether or not they have had puppies. When exposed to strong summer sunshine, the dark chocolate colour is known to fade towards ginger or yellow, somewhat patchily on the head and body. Hence, some owners keep them out of the sun to retain their colour, which is perhaps a little sad for the chocolate Labrador in a country where sunshine is at such a premium!

Yellow

These are the glamour boys and girls of the breed, made so popular over the past 30 years by the Andrex toilet tissue adverts on TV, featuring

The yellow colour varies in shade, with some Labradors being a pale cream.

Some yellow Labs are a deep, fox-red colour.

yellow Labrador puppies. The yellow Labrador coat colour ranges from pale cream to dark fox red.

The yellows make the most adorable pets, are top winners in the show ring, and work well in the shooting field. They have the best of temperaments (kindness itself), they are placid and extremely loving. Nothing fazes them. I often think their main thought is, "How's my hair looking today?" as they lazily smile and pat an ear with a paw. They are surely on this earth just to have a lovely, comfy life!

Yellows have the same double coat as the blacks and chocolates and, usually moult twice-yearly and bitches 19 weeks after their season. They also moult a tiny bit each day too. I am told the daily moult is because of the lack of black pigment in the hair follicles of the yellow coat.

In the end, perhaps your eventual decision on the colour of your chosen Labrador will come down to the basics of: Do you want yellow hairs on your navy suit or black or brown hairs in the butter?

The male (left) and the female (right) have minor differences in temperament.

DOG OR BITCH?

The choice of a male or female Labrador is very much a matter of personal preference, but there are a few points to consider.

Males

The Labrador male makes a lifelong, faithful, loveable friend. He is strong, jovial, hale and hearty, and loves his human family every single moment of his happy life. You will be his idol from the minute you meet.

At about 12 months of age he can become a bit of a silly teenager with eyes only for the girls, but this period is quickly over and he soon forgets the ladies, content to happily settle down to a life of pure devotion to his human family. Males grow to be larger and heavier than bitches; they are easy to train and make excellent family pets.

When a male puppy relieves himself, he will squat like a bitch. At around 10 months of age he will endeavour to start cocking his leg, a technique, that will bring you much mirth, as the skill takes a while to perfect and the starting attempts prove a bit inventive and wobbly! He will finally perfect his aim when he is around 12 months of age, at which time make sure you teach him never to cock his leg in the house or wherever he feels like it outside around the garden.

Castration: I do not believe a male Labrador needs to be castrated except on medical grounds. Speaking personally, and having entire male

Champion Labradors who have been used at stud, living here peacefully and happily to a ripe old age with all our bitches, I have yet to hear one good reason why the castration of a healthy, good-tempered male Labrador is a necessity. If the dogs are well mannered and trained properly in the first place then there should be no problem at all. However, others will argue in favour of castration, so it is a matter of seeking advice from your vet and from your puppy's breeder.

Bitches

Bitches are most endearing and they, too, make delightful pets. Neater and possibly more gentle and fastidious, they are smaller than the dogs, usually by about 50 mms at the shoulder. They therefore weigh less.

Seasons: Unspayed bitches come 'in season' or 'on heat' (ready for mating) once every six to eight months for a three-week period. The first season is usually when the bitch is around eight months of age, but it can be as late as two years. Yellow bitches are usually earlier in season than their black or chocolate littermates.

During the season the bitch may show a slight change in temperament and become slightly aloof (a bit like doggy PMT). She should not be taken off your property for exercise at this time, as there is always a risk that a loose male dog of unspecified parentage will appear out of the blue, and he will be only too pleased to quickly help himself to an impromptu mating!

Spaying of pet bitches: Bitches intended for the show ring or for breeding are not spayed. However, once a pet bitch has finished maturing (at around 18 months of age) and has had at least one previous season, you may consider spaying her. Your vet will remove the reproductive organs so that she will never come in season again, eradicating the risk of an unwanted pregnancy.

A plus point of spaying is that it can reduce the likelihood of mammary tumours later in life. The negative points of spaying are that it can bring about the growth of a heavy woolly coat, there is the possibility of weight gain, (which can be controlled by monitoring food intake), and, in a tiny number of cases, slight urinary leaking may occur in old age, but this is rare.

MORE THAN ONE?

Labradors love the company of other dogs. Two Labradors in a household are ideal. They keep each other company and are happy and contented when you are out. If you do aim to have two, just make sure that your first Labrador is at least two years of age before you take on the second. If your new Labrador is adult, too, consider introducing them on neutral ground – perhaps on a country walk, rather than in your home.

I would never advise acquiring two pups from the same litter or two pups of exactly the same age. The reason for this is that as they grow and get heavier, enthusiastic, under two-year-old Labradors can play very roughly with each other, albeit always in fun. They can charge around at great speed together, like motorcyclists in a race. These carefree games can get out of hand. The youngsters do not know their own strength and can easily crash into each other or fall awkwardly. A glancing collision at full gallop could well damage their growing joints, possibly causing lameness in later life.

My advice is to concentrate on rearing the first pup safely and correctly, and then, when he is about two to three years of age and much more steady and sensible, think about getting him a puppy companion.

At the other end of the age-scale, an old Labrador is rejuvenated by the arrival of a young puppy in his home.

Do not be tempted to get two puppies from the same litter – they will be twice the amount of work, and they will bond more closely with each other than with their family.

He takes on a completely new role in life as wise puppy-minder. He teaches the youngster the rules of the house and, in so doing, he himself becomes less sedate for finding a new reason for living.

BUYING A PUPPY

I would never advise buying a Labrador puppy from a pet shop or from a newspaper advert. Be suspicious of adverts that state "Can deliver" in which case you will never see the premises where the pup was raised or see his parents, if they really are the actual parents whose names appear on his possibly fictitious pedigree.

I would also be wary of selecting a Labrador breeder purely from a flashy website, unless you speak to the person in charge and later visit their premises to see the puppies with their mother.

It is also inadvisable to take on a puppy from your best friend's pet Labrador unless much thought has been put into the breeding of both parents. More often than not, the sire of the friend's litter is another pet dog, probably the cuddly, old yellow Lab, happy to oblige, from down the road. Unfortunately, it is unlikely that sire and dam conform to the Breed Standard or that they have ever been hip scored or eye tested. Your decision not to buy could avoid spoiling your friendship at a later date should things go wrong with the puppy. It is not worth the risk.

Health Screening

We are fortunate that the Labrador is a healthy breed and has relatively few breed-specific health issues. However, it's essential that the parents of your puppy are health checked. This includes scoring hips and possibly elbows, eye tests and DNA tests. When you go to see the breeder, ask to see the health certificates and check that the dates are current.

For detailed information see *Chapter Six: Health Care for Labradors.*

Buy the best puppy from the best breeder you can find.

FINDING A BREEDER

Your Labrador will be with you and your family for a very long time, and so you should be prepared to put time and effort into finding a puppy. Buyers travel the length and breadth of Britain to find their special puppy; your chosen breeder may not necessarily be the nearest Labrador kennel to your home address.

The Kennel Club has an excellent website, www.the-kennel-club.org.uk, where you will find details of KC Accredited Labrador breeders who have KC registered Labrador puppies available at the time. Alternatively, you can contact the Labrador breed clubs, which will have details of breeders with puppies available – all from health-checked parents.

Another source of information is the excellent website of *Our Dogs* weekly paper, which lists reputable Labrador breeders with puppies available from health-checked parents. Finally, ask your local vet if he could recommend a local Labrador breeder with quality Labrador puppies available; as always, they must be from health-checked parents.

ASSESSING THE LITTER

When you make contact with a breeder, you will need to discuss your requirements. It is important to state whether you want a show puppy, a working puppy or a pet. If you want a working dog, you will need to go to a specialist breeder, so it is important the breeder knows what you are looking for. Arrange to see the breeder when the puppies are about five weeks of age.

When you visit the breeder, you will also meet one or both of the health-checked parents at that time. In most cases, the father (sire) will not be on the premises, as the breeder will probably have travelled some distance to find the best stud dog for her bitch. The mother of the pups will be on the premises and will have performed the hard job feeding and cleaning up after her litter during the previous weeks. Hormonal changes after the birth may mean she is not in the best of coat when you visit, but she should appear bright-eyed, fit and well, and certainly not look dirty, drained, exhausted or thin. In all likelihood, she will greet you with her tail wagging happily and be proud to show you her lovely babies.

When you arrive, the puppies may be playing or they may be fast asleep. They should be living in clean conditions and, once awake, they should appear bright eyed, happy, and look you straight in the eye,

The breeder will need to make sure that you can provide a suitable home for one of their precious puppies.

which is a sign of good, honest character. They should be alert and inquisitive with none holding back timorously in the corner. They will have been wormed twice already so should look healthy and well rounded.

The breeder will ask you lots of questions about your home and lifestyle. Do not be offended – a responsible breeder will have put a great deal of care and effort into rearing the puppies and will want them to go to reliable, permanent homes where there is no risk that the puppy will become surplus to requirements and returned to be rehomed at a later date.

The questions you will need to answer will range over many aspects including the following:

• Do all the members of the household want a dog?
• Are you in a position to care for, feed and exercise a Labrador properly?
• Are you away from the house for long periods each day?
• Is there a garden, which is well fenced, up to a height of at least 5 ft (1.5 m), ensuring the puppy cannot escape?
• Does any member of the household have allergies to dogs?
• Where will the puppy sleep at night and during the day if you have to go out?

The breeder must be completely satisfied that the puppy's future well-being will be assured, before he or she allows you to book a puppy, which will mean paying a deposit.

CHOOSING A PUP WITH SHOW POTENTIAL

If you have told the breeder you wish to show your puppy, my best advice is to allow the breeder to select your show puppy. It is most unlikely that all the puppies in the litter will be show quality. Those who are will stand out when the breeder examines their conformation at around seven weeks of age and watches them move and play day by day.

What does the experienced breeder look for in a show puppy? In the first place, a show puppy has a certain style about the way he holds himself when moving. He needs an extrovert character, a perfect temperament, and really must have that X Factor!

It takes an expert eye to assess show potential.

Settling In

Once your Labrador puppy or adult is booked, you have about three weeks to sort out all the practical things needing attention around your house and garden before he arrives.

IN THE GARDEN

Labradors are intelligent, inquisitive dogs, who usually think one step ahead of you. Your garden must be well fenced and totally secure, with no escape holes in the boundary fence. You do not want your new Labrador to disappear across the road, or to chase next door's cat in his very first minutes with you.

An inquisitive puppy will explore his new surroundings so you need to ensure the environment is 100 per cent safe and secure.

Labradors can clear medium-height fences quite easily, if they are so inclined. The garden fence should be at least 5-6 ft high (1.5-1.8 metres); ideally, a close-boarded wooden fence on concrete, or stout wooden posts. Do not use chain-link fencing, as it is easy to unravel. You will also need to check that side gates are protected at the sides and at the bottom. Remember, it only takes a split second for a puppy to get out and be run over by a passing car.

You should also check that foxes have not taken up residence in your garden, as they can spread mange to dogs. If you are suspicious that you may have unwelcome guests, call your local council for help.

Toilet area

Select a designated toilet area for your Labrador to use in the garden. Purchase a suitable bucket and shovel, or use a polythene bag to remove faeces as and when it appears during the day.

Ponds and swimming pools

Fence off all pools! Surround your ornamental fishponds, swimming pools and water features with wire netting on sturdy posts, otherwise you will find your Labrador enjoying a dip!

With regards to straight-sided swimming pools and fish-ponds, while an adult Labrador will enjoy swimming in the water and may or may not be able to get out, a puppy will most certainly drown if he falls in unsupervised and cannot climb up the vertical sides to safety.

Sheds, cold-frames and greenhouses

The garden shed is usually home to expensive equipment, sharp tools, dangerous chemicals, slug bait, rat poison, weed-killers, paint etc. Make sure that the door can be firmly bolted and is closed at all times. Store any hazardous items at a high level, just in case someone leaves the door open by mistake.

If you have a greenhouse or glass cold-frame in a prominent central position, put temporary low-level wooden boarding across the exposed glass sides, so that when your Labrador goes charging around in play, he doesn't go crashing through the glass whilst he's busy showing off and not watching where he is going.

Poisonous plants and garden chemicals

Make sure there are no poisonous plants, such as Euphorbias or monkshood, in the borders, and ensure that cocoa mulch has never been used anywhere, as it is very poisonous to dogs. Remove anything suspicious and dispose at the local council tip.

Slug pellets are lethal. Never use them in the garden if you own a dog. Even the pet-repellent ones appear to attract inquisitive Labradors looking for something to taste. Weedkillers on lawns and paths must be dry before your dog walks over the treated area, as the pads of his feet could absorb the poison.

You may decide to restrict access to certain parts of the house.

Choosing A Name

Think of a good pet name for your dog. Make it short, probably two syllables, and easy to call out when on a walk. Be careful: sometimes you wish you had chosen another name. I had a Lab called Barclay, who barked a lot, and another called Digger, who dug holes in the lawn!

Rats and water bowls

Never leave your dog's drinking water outside over night. Rats carry leptospirosis, which can be contracted when un-inoculated dogs drink water in which rats have urinated.

IN THE HOME

Decide which rooms in the house your Labrador is going to occupy. A puppy is best kept downstairs in the kitchen/utility room until he is house trained. Upstairs is a no-go area for a puppy. He must not be allowed to climb stairs until his bones are mature; at least over 12 months old.

An adult Labrador might be allowed the freedom of the house, but do remember that he is likely to be a big dog whose legs, paws and under-body will often get very wet and muddy during exercise. He will certainly need drying off and cleaning with a towel before being allowed into the sitting room.

I would suggest you keep your Labrador out of rooms containing valuable antiques; one swipe of his happily wagging tail could cause an expensive disaster if he sweeps the Dresden ornaments on to the floor; and the odd nibble of an original Chippendale chair leg might prove somewhat unpopular, too!

Once you have selected the rooms to be used, put all remaining valuable items up high, out of reach. Keep him away from the computer and its ancillary bits and bobs. Remove mobile phones, spectacle cases and remote controls for TVs,

DVDs and videos. Labradors find all these a joy to retrieve and crunch!

In areas where your Lab passes through, make sure there are no accessible electric cables left plugged in and switched on. Clear up abandoned shoes, socks and clothing, which may be lying around the house. Many a sock has travelled the length of a Labrador's digestive system. This can prove fatal.

Finally, where food is concerned, a reminder that Labradors believe in the 'help yourself' method, having little conscience in this department. Make sure the fridge, pantry door, and kitchen cupboards are all firmly shut and your grocery shopping bags are out of reach. Keep the dishwasher closed. Labradors have been known to climb in, turn round and clean the dishes themselves! If he learns to open lever door-handles, to the pantry for example, replace the handles with circular doorknobs!

Dishwasher tablets, drain cleaning fluid and washing powder are all very poisonous. Keep them well away from your dog.

Locating an indoor crate

If you are bringing a puppy home, as opposed to an adult, he will be living downstairs in his crate for some of the time. Decide where you would like the crate to go. He will not be house trained at this point. To become well socialised, he will need to live in the hub of the family, not left in an isolated room, far away from all the daily goings-on; ideally, the kitchen or utility room are best, with quick access to the back door to aid initial toilet training.

Do not site the indoor kennel in a glass conservatory, unless it is well ventilated and fully shaded – otherwise, even with the windows open, it will be dangerously hot in summer and too cold in the winter. If you are buying an indoor kennel for an adult, site this in the kitchen, utility or living room, so that he can be with you as much as possible.

BUYING EQUIPMENT

You can purchase most equipment you need from your nearest pet store, pet supermarket, or on-line.

Indoor kennel/crate

Your Labrador will love his very own wire-mesh, indoor dog crate, which most of the time will have the door open. The crate is his own private bedroom, a place where he can take all his toys and trophies; somewhere no one else can invade.

The easily dismantled wire crate has a removable, plastic tray in the base. The smallest size crate for a Labrador is 24 ins by 37 ins by 27 ins (61 x 94 x 69 cms), and the crate usually has two opening doors.

Puppy playpen

If you have space, you may wish to buy a puppy playpen. Sturdily made from several 3-ft-high (90 cm) by 3- or 4-ft-wide (90 or 120 cm) interlinked wire panels, including an opening door, it has a removable, rigid plastic base tray. The playpen, which can be easily dismantled, allows the puppy a safe, controlled play area. It will only be usable in the first four months, after which he will probably find he can climb out, so regard the playpen as a useful short-term training aid. (It can thereafter be used as a surround to protect the plants in the garden!)

Stairgate

Purchase a stairgate for the bottom of the stairs if your adult Labrador is not to be allowed upstairs. Adult Labradors quickly learn how to open simple catches on stairgates, so purchase one with a flip over, locking catch, operated by depressing two safety buttons.

Dog beds

These come in spectacular shapes and sizes. Young puppies often test their teeth out on their beds, so do not waste money buying an expensive bed at this stage. For a puppy, either use a 24-inch (60 cm) plastic puppy bed, or a large cardboard box (remove metal staples or any sticky tape). You can replace

There is a wide range of dog equipment available, but to begin with it is best to concentrate on the essentials.

the cardboard box as it gets grubby, chewed up or squashed. Once the puppy is fully-grown, buy him an easily cleaned, adult plastic dog bed. The minimum size needed is 27 by 18 ins (69 x 46 cms).

Do not be tempted into buying a foam-filled bed, even though they look very cosy. A Labrador will chew through it in no time, and then swallow the foam, which could have disastrous consequences.

Bedding

You will need at least three pieces of synthetic fleece bedding so that there is always some available while the rest is in the wash or drying. Dog bedding should be regularly washed in the washing machine with non-biological powder, as biological powder can cause skin irritation.

Bowls and buckets

A Labrador's favourite trick is to pick up his bowl and wander around with it in his mouth. Therefore, choose unbreakable, stainless-steel bowls; fancy crockery bowls do not survive long when dropped on the tiled kitchen floor.

You will need at least three stainless-steel feeding bowls 8-10 ins (20-25 cms) in diameter, preferably with cone-shaped sides and non-slip bottom rim. Because of the conical shape, your Labrador is unlikely to pick these bowls up.

A 9-inch (22.5-cm) stainless-steel water pail, which can be sited outdoors during the day (except in frosty weather), is also a good investment. Bring the water pail in at night, as previously mentioned.

Remember all bowls should be washed thoroughly after use.

Collar and lead

An eight-week-old puppy will not have been lead trained. However, when you collect him, take a 15-inch (38-cm) soft, nylon puppy collar and a non-leather lead, just in case you have any problems with the car breaking down during the journey home and you need to take the puppy out of the car for any length of time.

You will need to ensure your puppy has an ID tag attached to his collar.

He will outgrow this small collar very quickly. Do not buy an expensive leather collar and lead at this stage, as he will probably chew it up.

It is dangerous to leave a collar on a young Labrador while he is running free unsupervised in your own garden. If a sturdy branch of a shrub gets caught through the collar while the puppy is speeding past, it could easily break his neck.

For a well-trained adult Labrador, a rounded leather collar or plain nylon collar, usually around 24-26 ins (60-66 cms) long, and a leather lead are ideal. Extending/retractable leads are also very useful. These enable dogs to have controlled running exercise in areas where they are not allowed off the lead.

Toys

From puppyhood through to old age, your Labrador will amuse himself with tennis balls, squeaky toys, rubber rings, plastic dumbbells, rope tugs, Kongs, and empty plastic bottles – all are sources of play and enjoyment.

Soft toys are available in plenty from charity shops. Make sure they are safe for very young children, in which case they will suit your dog, otherwise removable parts, such as glass eyes, could be detached and swallowed.

Car accessories

Just as the law requires passengers in the rear of a vehicle to wear seat belts, so it is not advisable to have a dog travelling loose behind the driver.

A Labrador puppy will love whatever toys you give him.

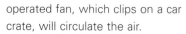
Should there be a collision 70 lbs (32 kgs) of loose Labrador catapulted forward could cause serious harm to the driver – and the dog may well go through the windscreen.

A purpose-made car crate for your particular vehicle or a standard-sized car crate ensures everyone is safe. If there is no room for a crate, try a travel harness, which secures in the rear seatbelt restraints, or fix a dog guard specific for your vehicle between the front and rear seats.

Window shades will help keep the back of the car cooler for your dog on hot sunny days, and a battery-operated fan, which clips on a car crate, will circulate the air.

Tough, washable boot liners and seat covers are worth considering for the days when you need to transport a muddy Labrador.

COLLECTING YOUR LABRADOR

At last, the big day has arrived and it is time to collect your Labrador. The breeder should have already discussed with you the items you need to assemble prior to the pick-up date, and you should have them ready to hand.

Getting ready

Before you go to get him, set up the crate ready. Cover the plastic base tray with plenty of newspaper. A puppy will also need a medium-sized cardboard box or a plastic puppy bed, in which you have placed more paper and the machine-washable fleece bedding or old blanket.

Arrange to collect the puppy or adult in the morning, as opposed to late afternoon. In the summer it will be cooler and it gives him several hours to get to know you before he goes to sleep on his first night in his new home. If you are collecting a puppy, take a friend with you to hold, comfort and steady him, while he sits on a towel on their lap. The puppy will probably drop off to sleep during the

After all the hard work of rearing a litter, it is time for the breeder to say goodbye to the puppies.

journey. If you are on your own, use a dog crate to transfer the puppy or adult. If no crate is available, borrow one from a friend. Never travel on your own with a puppy loose in the car.

Paperwork

At collection time, a reputable breeder will give you the puppy's detailed rearing instructions. These will include a diet sheet, how much exercise the puppy should receive, and how to start lead and house training. Much care will have been put into raising the puppy since birth and the breeder will expect you to continue the process.

You will receive a copy of the pup's Kennel Club registration certificate and a copy of his four- or five-generation pedigree. The pedigree is the puppy's family tree, with Champions printed in red. Included in the puppy pack will be copies of the health certificates of both parents.

Insurance cover, which normally covers any unexpected vet bills or the loss of your puppy during the first six weeks in your home, will also be provided.

You will also be given a contract of sale to sign. Read this carefully, as it may include conditions, such as not being permitted to breed your Labrador. Responsible breeders will also state that the pup should be returned to them if circumstances change and the pup needs rehoming.

ARRIVING HOME

Whether you have decided on an adult Labrador, a rescued dog or a puppy, do not overwhelm him with too many visitors when he first arrives home. He needs to settle in quietly and get his bearings. If the puppy or adult is shy, do not over-face him; leave him be for the time being.

Offer him a drink of water, then show him around the garden and take him to his designated toilet spot. After a while, give him his first dinner. Food is the way to a Labrador's heart. He will probably forget all his apprehension, gobble his dinner, and, from then on, be your best pal – completely won over by your whole family, who deliver such gorgeous meals!

During the changeover period, make sure you stick to the food the breeder has given you, otherwise his tummy may become upset. If you do change the food for whatever reason, take several days to do so, gradually mixing the new food in with the old food.

For information on feeding, see Chapter Four: Caring for your Labrador.

Children in the family will be very excited by the new arrival, but they

Interaction between a puppy and a small child should be carefully supervised.

the puppy has very sharp teeth and scratchy claws and to keep their faces and fingers well away from the puppy.

Do not let children torment the puppy by holding him down and tickling his feet or pulling his ears or tail. If things get too exuberant, put the puppy in his crate for a while with a treat.

Before eating food, after playing with the puppy, ensure the children wash their hands.

Do not let your puppy assume he can climb on to your lap every day by right – he will still want to do it when he is fully grown, which is a rather different prospect...

MEETING RESIDENT PETS

When introducing two adult dogs it is better to do this outside in the garden or on neutral territory away from home, so arrange to 'accidentally' meet up on a pleasant walk. With the new Labrador on his lead, make a great fuss of your existing dog as you introduce them. Remember not to make the resident dog jealous; he must receive most of the love and attention plus a few extra treats. They may have the odd grump at each other, but within a couple of weeks, the hierarchy will have been sorted out between them and they should be firm friends. Avoid leaving them together, unattended, before this time.

should be encouraged to be calm so as not to frighten him. Let them pat and stroke him gently, but no squealing. A puppy should be held firmly on a parent's lap for the children to stroke. Never allow youngsters to pick up a puppy; he will be too heavy, will wriggle and go crashing to the floor. Make sure the children play with the pup while they are sitting on the floor and not standing up. Make them aware that

When introducing a puppy, do not let him make free with the other pet's toys, bed or food, and never leave the puppy with an older dog at this introduction stage. In the early months do not allow the puppy to run freely with adult dogs. They tend to play far too roughly and delight in running puppies down, causing possible bone damage.

The resident cat may or may not take to your new Labrador. The cat will be very aloof initially. Do not leave the new puppy with a cat, as the pup will be inquisitive and is likely to come off worse in any argument. Eyes can be badly damaged, so extra vigilance is needed. As long as the cat can keep his dignity, escape out of the way without being chased, ensure his bed is not taken and his dinner is not stolen by the impudent young Labrador, the pair will become great friends, eventually snuggling up together on chilly nights.

THE FIRST NIGHT

During the day, the puppy will have met everyone, eaten, played and, hopefully, toileted outside, so he should be tired by bedtime. Put newspaper on the crate floor and settle him in his crate with his water bowl or tiny stainless-steel bucket secured so it cannot be tipped over, a biscuit to chew, and the door finally closed for the night.

A radio turned on low or a loud ticking alarm-clock may help him to feel that he has not been abandoned; a hot-water bottle or heated pad under his blanket in his bed will also make him relax. After the experiences of such a busy day, he may drop off to sleep and only wake when you appear at breakfast time. On the other hand, he may howl plaintively non-stop for a few hours. He may feel utterly sad and dejected, lonely and chilly, being on his own for the very first time without his brothers and

A puppy has to learn to settle at night without the warmth and comfort of his littermates.

sisters to keep him snug.

It is very difficult to harden your heart and ignore his cries. Ideally, you should do this, but most owners will end up leaving their warm bed upstairs to go down to comfort the sad little fellow, who, in turn, thinks: "Wow, this is great! If I want to see my owner in the middle of the night, all I've got to do is howl a bit louder!"

If you cannot bear the sound of his cries, for this first night only, take his crate upstairs and set it up beside your bed. Carry the puppy upstairs and put him in the crate. He should sleep soundly then. Do not take him into your bed; you could roll on him and squash him. The next night you really must ignore his cries and make him sleep downstairs on his own. He will soon get used to it.

The more vigilant you are, the quicker your puppy will be to get the idea of house training.

HOUSE TRAINING

This is easy and your puppy will usually get the idea of what is required within the first three days. Your Labrador puppy will be used to using newspaper in his toilet area. Once he comes to live with you, the newspaper should be spread by the back door. Puppy training pads are also available, which can be placed by the door instead of newspaper. As he gets used to using the paper or pads, open the back door and move the paper outside.

On waking, after eating, and after a play session, your puppy will want to relieve himself. Take him outside to the spot in the garden you have chosen for his toilet. We say "Hurry up" to encourage him. When he goes, give him lots of praise and he will very soon get the message.

There are bound to be accidents. If you witness the accident, scold him with a gruff voice ("No, outside!") and take him outside immediately. If you are not there when he has an accident, do not scold him when you finally do see what has happened. He will not remember what he has done and will not understand why his lovely owner is so cross.

If your puppy gets excited, he will also want to relieve himself. Watch out for the pup darting around rapidly in circles and possibly squeaking, usually after a period of play. This is a sure sign that he wants to go outside, in which case, scoop him up immediately and take him outside to the toilet spot. Praise any results lavishly.

At night, your puppy will sleep in his bed in his crate with the door shut. His water bowl or pail will be in the crate with him. Dogs and puppies do not like to foul their crates, and, because of this, he will house train easily. If he squeaks to go to the toilet, put him outside. Praise him when he has been and put him back in the crate with a treat, so he builds up a good association with the crate.

TAKE-CARE REMINDERS

There are a few important things to be aware of in your puppy's early days with you:

- Before his vaccinations are complete, do not let adult dogs from other households meet him. When attending the vet's for his vaccinations, keep him either in the car or on your knee in the reception area. Do not put him down on the floor where poorly dogs may have been.
- Do not let him jump in and out of your car, especially if it has a high rear floor, such as in a 4 x 4. Lift him.
- Do not allow him to climb up and down stairs or climb big doorsteps, as these can damage developing limbs.
- He must not jump on and off furniture, or slide about on tiled floors.
- If he has been sitting on your lap, when you stand up, hold him tightly to put him on the ground. Make sure all his four feet are in contact with the floor before you release him and stand up.
- In the growing period, all games must be gentle; sudden lurching around is not good for the puppy's growing frame.
- When you are not there to supervise him, the puppy is far safer left shut in his crate.

Taking on a puppy is a big responsibility, so make sure you adhere to the 'take care' reminders.

Caring For A Labrador

The Labrador is such an easy dog to own and care for. With his bright eyes, smiley face, and adorable character, he brings out the very best in everyone he meets. If he comes from health-checked parents, he is likely to be a healthy, sound dog. He will probably only visit the vet for initial vaccinations at eight and 10 weeks of age; followed 12 months later by his annual check-up and booster. Other than these occasional visits and unexpected emergencies, his life should be almost vet-free.

The Labrador is an active breed that needs a good-quality, well-balanced diet.

The secrets of giving a Labrador a long and healthy life are:

- Rear him correctly in his first year, following the breeder's written instructions to the letter.
- Feed him properly during his growing phase.
- Do not over-exercise him before he is 18 months of age, at which time his bones should have finished growing and be fully calcified.
- Control his intake of food throughout adulthood. Do ensure he has a slight waistline.
- Labradors can stand low temperatures, but not draughts, so make sure he has a suitable, comfy place to rest and sleep.
- Keep him clean and well groomed, regularly inspecting his ears, teeth and nails.
- Train him to be an obedient, well-mannered dog, who will do you credit.
- Consult the breeder with any queries you may have about your Labrador during his life.

DIET AND NUTRITION

Labradors will eat anything you chose to feed them. They are not fussy eaters, so there is a great choice open to you with regards to what to purchase. These days, supermarkets and pet outlets stock their own-labels and well-known brands of all-in-one and 'tinned' dog food. On-line ordering for home delivery is also available to save carrying heavy sacks.

The selection of dry food from different manufacturers is enormous and this has become the staple diet of the majority of Labradors worldwide. All-in-one complete diets take the guesswork out of feeding, having all the necessary protein, vitamins and minerals added for each life stage. Its crunchiness ensures teeth are always clean and strong, too.

Some breeders still feed tripe and wholemeal biscuit. It smells, but the dogs love it. Tripe can easily cause weight increase if fed too generously. Other dog owners feed minced, cooked beef, which is available to buy frozen in bulk and fed with biscuit.

In this age of questioning processed products and the possibility of health problems they might cause, the BARF diet has evolved. Biologically Appropriate Raw Food is gaining popularity and whole chickens and bones are fed to, and enjoyed by, dogs. This is something I have never done, being too concerned about the bones perforating the gut, but those Labrador breeders who do use the BARF diet find it really suits their dogs and is very economical if there is a chicken-processing plant nearby.

In the end, as you will soon find out, your Labrador will appreciate whatever food you give him!

FEEDING REGIMES

As Labrador 'clocks' are very accurate, never do anything at the same time each day, otherwise he will expect you to be there, bang on time, every single day. This includes feeding time. If you establish a regular set feeding time, exactly five minutes before that time he may annoyingly start to bark. This is to remind you that, in case you had forgotten, dinner time is fast approaching and you ought to get your skates on! Therefore, I suggest you feed at a slightly different time each day.

Feeding a puppy

When you collect your puppy at eight weeks of age he will be having four regularly spaced meals daily, at around 7.30am, 12 noon, 5pm and 9pm. Each meal of dry puppy food will weigh around 2.5 to 3 oz. (65-75 gm). As he grows, the meals will increase in quantity but decrease in number. Water should always be available.

When he is about 12 weeks of age, you may find your puppy starts to pick at his fourth, final meal of the day, perhaps preferring to play instead of clearing his dish. This is the time to cut out the final evening meal and increase the amount fed at the other three meals.

Continue to feed the daily weight of food for his age as advised on the product bag, but now divide the amount into three meals instead of four, giving a small biscuit at bed-time instead. In a similar manner, when he is about six months of age, the lunchtime meal may be dropped. From then onwards, feed two meals a day, one at breakfast and the other at tea time.

Always use the amounts printed on the product bag as a rough guide, but also watch his waistline; he should be neither too fat nor too thin, so cut back or increase the amount fed in order to visually maintain his correct shape and size. *Always weigh the food; do not guess.*

It is important that no additional supplements should be added to an all-in-one balanced food; this could cause bone-growth abnormalities.

Food for adults

Once he is adult, your Labrador's dietary requirements are pretty basic. The Labrador is a good-doer and while he will always heartily appreciate whatever food you put down for him to eat, it is not necessary for you to buy the most expensive brand of food on the market; a mid-priced one will do very well.

Your Labrador's breeder or rescue charity will have given you details of what food is most suitable. Most proprietary brands of dry dog food

are available in a balanced age-specific range: puppy, junior (for growing dogs), adult, senior and working. Your adult Labrador may have one or two meals daily - a total, on average, of between 12-18 oz (300-510 gm) per day (some Labs need more, some less). Moisten the food with cold water immediately before it is fed, which prevents your Labrador swallowing the food too quickly. He will also enjoy a bone-shaped or oval biscuit for breakfast and at bedtime.

As with a puppy, any changes to his diet must be carried out over several days to avoid tummy upsets.

DANGERS OF OBESITY

Labradors love food. Owners love their Labradors and some express that great love by falling for their Labrador's pleading looks. What happens? They give him just one more tasty treat, then perhaps another, and another, as he really did enjoy the first so much. The trouble

Take the guessing out of feeding and weigh food at every mealtime.

A Labrador will do his very best to persuade you that he needs extra food.

This is not to say that too thin is good, either. Your dog should neither be too fat nor too thin. You should be able to feel each individual rib beneath the skin and flesh covering his ribcage, but you should not be able to see the lines of his ribs – if you can, he is too thin. Another good test to check if he is too fat is to feel his brisket, between his front legs. In a dog of the correct weight, there should be no excess flesh and certainly none hanging down.

BONES

If you wish to give your Labrador a bone, provide a large, fresh marrowbone (cooked ones splinter and they can swallow the dangerously sharp bits). Scrape most of the very rich marrow fat out of a fresh bone with a spoon and give the bone for only around 30 minutes, otherwise he will grind the whole thing up, swallow it all and make himself very sick for the next 24 hours.

is that unless the calorific value of the treats is deducted from his daily food allowance – which is not likely to happen – treats become excess food and this excess is stored as body fat. A fat Labrador will most likely have health problems and a shorter life than one of the correct weight.

Foods To Avoid

- Never give your Labrador large, bone-shaped hide chews. Many Labradors have died swallowing these whole. Sadly, once in the gut, they absorb moisture, expand, and can cause a complete blockage, which the vet usually finds impossible to remove.
- Do not feed cows' milk; older puppies and adult Labradors cannot digest the lactose.
- Do not feed chocolate, which contains theobromine, a substance highly poisonous to dogs. It only takes 7oz/200gms of dark chocolate to kill a Labrador. For the same reason, do not use cocoa mulch in the garden, as this also contains theobromine
- Grapes and raisins can be highly poisonous to dogs.
- Dogs may be extremely allergic to products containing Xylitol (such as sugar-free gum).

GROOMING

The Labrador's coat is easy to care for. He has a thick, double coat, consisting of a waterproof topcoat, which repels dirt, and a warm, thick undercoat. To keep him healthy and well groomed, a daily brush with a stiff dandy brush will spruce up his coat and remove any dried mud. Do not try to brush wet mud off the coat; wait until it is dry. You can use a wide-toothed comb and a narrow-toothed comb to remove dead hairs.

After a wet walk, use a towel to dry him off, and, once dry, rub him all over with a piece of kitchen towel to remove grease and dirt and then use a damp wash-leather to make him sparkle.

For the twice-yearly moult,

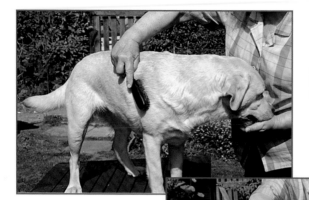

A daily brush will keep your Labrador's coat in good order.

A shedding rake works wonders when your Labrador is moulting.

consider buying a shedding rake. The shedding rake must be used very carefully, as it could scratch the skin if used roughly. However, it does work wonderfully well, removing clouds of dead undercoat, which, in summer, can be spread around the hosta plants in the garden to stop the snails munching them to bits. It works!

Nail care

Inspect your Labrador's nails on regular basis to make sure they are not long or curled. This is especially important with older dogs. When a Labrador has the correct-shaped feet, his nails automatically wear level as he walks on hard road surfaces and will not need much trimming. However, if he is only exercised on grass, or he has long, open toes, you may need to trim his nails every few weeks.

I use guillotine nail clippers, which are ideal for Labrador claws. Make sure you do not cut into the quick, the blood-filled part of the claw, which bleeds profusely if nicked in error. Causing a nail to bleed will hurt your Lab – and the next time he

Nails will need trimming, including the dew claw – the dog's 'thumb'.

A daily wipe with a moist tissue will keep eyes free from debris.

spies you with the nail clippers, he will be off to hide under the table!

The correct procedure is to thread each nail through the hole in the clipper. Note the position of the quick (not always easy on a black nail) and hold the paw steady as the cutting blade passes over the end of the claw, away from the quick, removing only the pointed excess. Ask someone to hold the dog's head while you trim the nails. You will also need to trim the dewclaws, (the dog's thumbs) on the side of his legs, once again avoiding the quick.

Eye care

Your Labrador's eyes should be clear and bright. A daily wipe of the inner corner with a tissue is all that is required. Ask the vet to check if you see any redness of the white of the eye, sagging of the eyelid below the eye, or signs of conjunctivitis.

Ear inspection

Check your Labrador's ears on a weekly basis to ensure they are clean and odour-free. There are many proprietary ear cleaners and ear wipes available from pet shops. However, I believe the less you put down the dog's ears, the better. A weekly wipe with a tissue or moist cotton wool should suffice to remove any dirt. Do not poke cotton-buds down the dog's ears as you could inflict damage.

Clean the ears, but do not probe into the ear canal.

If you feed a soft diet, you will need to clean teeth on a regular basis.

Some Labradors have narrow ear canals, which can be the site of fungal ear infections, or they may get ear mites, usually passed on by a cat. In this situation, a dog will either scratch his ear, hold his head on one side, or shake it violently. These signs, and the appearance of black wax, tell you that specialised ear cleaners and ear drops from your vet are required. Never let ear problems go unattended.

Dental care

Labradors with full dentition have 42 strong, white teeth, which appear to stay in good condition all their lives, with little tartar build-up. Some Labradors lack full dentition; a few premolars just never grow in when the adult teeth appear. In Europe this is regarded as a major fault, but in Britain feelings are more relaxed as long as the scissor bite is correct. (This means that the teeth on the upper jaw should closely overlap the teeth on the lower jaw.) In fact, shooting men of former times regarded missing premolars as no problem, saying in that case there were fewer teeth to damage the birds that the Labradors retrieved!

Eating dried food and gnawing bones seems to aid tooth cleansing. If you decide to feed a softer diet, you will probably need to attend to his teeth more often. If you need to clean your Labrador's teeth, doggy toothpaste and finger-worn doggy toothbrushes are available at pet stores. If, however, the teeth become heavily encrusted with tartar, this must be removed under sedation by a vet, otherwise gum disease and subsequent tooth loss may occur.

BATHTIME

Although I have hot and cold taps installed outside precisely for occasional dog bathing, it is seldom necessary to bath a Labrador. Most people use the shower over the indoor bath to bathe their dog. If you do wish to give your Labrador a bath, you should appreciate that it can be a very wet occupation.

Bear in mind that bathing makes the Labrador's coat very soft

Exercise should be limited while a Labrador is still growing.

for five days. If you intend to show him, bath him at least one week before the show so that the coat returns to its normal harsh-to-the-touch texture before the event.

It is also worth remembering that your Labrador will try to find the grubbiest of places to roll after his bath in a bid to rid himself of that horrid clean smell...

EXERCISE FOR YOUNG LABRADORS

Labrador puppies are full of energy and fun, but they must not be over-exercised in their first year. Their growing bones do not calcify until they are fully mature. Once the

bones have fully calcified, exercise may be given freely. However, it cannot be emphasised too strongly that if a puppy is over-exercised before that time, permanent damage could well be done to the skeletal frame, possibly harming the hips, hocks or elbows. This type of injury means that your Lab may well become arthritic in later life.

Before vaccinations are complete at 12-14 weeks, the puppy cannot go out and it is advisable not to have other dogs in his vicinity, if they are being exercised in public places. Up to six months of age, he needs very little exercise apart from a run around your well-fenced garden. It is worthwhile taking the puppy in the car to socialise him at shops and outside schools, but no long walks.

From 6 to 12 months of age, he can gradually be given more gentle exercise on the lead, aiming for two miles daily at 12 months.

From 12 to 18 months, exercise can be increased until you can take your Labrador wherever you wish to go – short walks or long walks – for the rest of his life.

Remember, never exercise your Labrador in the full midday sun; wait until it is cool.

PLAYING GAMES

Labrador puppies need lots of food and sleep in their first few months, interspersed with gentle playtime and plenty of love. They are lively; the owner must dictate the manner

Combining a game of retrieve with a play in water is a Labrador's idea of heaven.

of play, otherwise the pup will simply career around to the point of exhaustion.

Your puppy is like a human toddler. His bones are soft and still growing for at least 18 months. Treat him as you would a toddler. No rough play. Although he will naturally retrieve, do not be tempted to throw things too far for him; exercise should be very gentle with no violent galloping or turning, which could ruin his growing joints.

The best things to play with are tennis balls, squeaky toys, rope twists and, later, when the dog is older, a Kong. (This is not good for young puppies as the Kong's unusual bouncing can encourage the pup to twist awkwardly at speed.)

Adult Labradors love to play for hours on end and will happily retrieve anything you care to throw. Old tennis balls are ideal, but never throw sticks or stones, as the former can damage the back of the dog's throat and the latter may break his teeth or be swallowed.

It is not a good ideal to allow your Lab to play with a football. He will career around so roughly with it that he could end up either lame or with damaged toes.

If you are buying a rubber ball, ensure there is either no hole in it, or that there are at least two holes in it to prevent a vacuum forming should the dog's tongue gets stuck through the hole. There have been dreadful accidents with Labs getting their tongues stuck in the single hole and subsequently requiring drastic veterinary treatment.

CAR TRAVEL

A Labrador loves to be included in every outing – even if it is simply a trip out in the car. However, in hot weather, cars can be death traps for dogs.

Do not take your Labrador in the car if there is any chance at all that you will have to leave your car parked in the sunshine – even for five minutes.

It is important to provide a safe and secure accommodation in the car.

Leaving a crack of car window open is no good at all. Your dog is far better left at home in his crate.

The temperature in a car parked in sun rises so rapidly that dogs will die within 20 minutes; the internal organs start to cook in the heat, which can reach 150 degrees Fahrenheit. Within minutes the dog dies a horrible, painful death. This is entirely preventable.

CARING FOR THE OLDER LABRADOR

Labradors are classed as veterans in the show ring from the age of seven. However, most will still be very sprightly until well past 10 years. As he approaches his teen years, while he will still enjoy his daily walk, he may become a little slower, and, on his return home will seek his warm, comfortable bed in which to doze away the rest of the day, before his still eagerly awaited evening meal.

With his exercise reduced, watch your Labrador's waistline; he does not want to be carrying excess weight. Be prepared to cut his nails, including dewclaws, frequently. With less exercise, his nails will grow very quickly. When dewclaws are left untrimmed they can curl right round and grow into his leg. Toenails that are too long will also cause him to walk very badly.

Labradors, just like humans, can have strokes, which at first may look fatal but which often are not. Do not be too hasty. Just because your dog has had a stroke doesn't necessarily mean he has to be put down on the day of the stroke. If he regains consciousness, even though he is walking beside a wall at a peculiar angle, wait four or five days; more often than not, he will have revived completely by the end of this time. He may live many months or even years longer with no further occurrence.

The older Labrador often grows the odd fatty tumour somewhere on his body, usually on his side. They are large, hard, round lumps growing directly under the skin or muscle, up to the size of half a grapefruit. Do not be alarmed: although they may look rather odd, they usually prove non-malignant under veterinary examination. As long as the lumps do not impair the dog's mobility. they are best left alone and not removed. The fewer anaesthetics and operations an elderly dog is subject to, the better. Do, of course, get any lump checked out by your vet, to ensure the growth is not malignant. If a tumour is malignant, it must be removed by your vet promptly.

Old age often brings with it the same problems applicable to dogs as to humans: deafness, sore gums, rotting or worn teeth, failing eyesight, sore feet, tender limbs and an intolerance of youngsters! Keep his ears and eyes clean and check his teeth. Be sympathetic with him and make his last few years comfortable – he has served you well and, until now, has asked little in return.

Eventually, the day will come when you have to steel yourself to say a final goodbye to your dear old Labrador. Perhaps he is in constant pain from inoperable cancer or arthritis; maybe he refuses his food; his hind legs have become unable to support him, or he is totally incontinent, something he will hate.

You need to be aware of the changing needs of your Labrador as he grows older.

However many Labradors you own, the final deed will break your heart. In extreme old age, 12 years onwards, while his decline may have happened over a period of months, you may find that one day your Labrador is as well as usual, and the next he shows signs of being very poorly indeed. His health can change very quickly.

When I am faced with this situation, I ask myself if he is

affected by any one of the following, and if the answer is "Yes", I believe the horrible time to say goodbye has probably come, and, very reluctantly, I ring for the vet, who will make the final decision.

The sure signs of decline in a Labrador are:-

• Disinclination to eat.
• Unable to eat or drink without being sick
• Incontinent and unable to raise himself to go outside to the toilet.
• Unable to raise himself off his bed to walk about.
• Back legs unable to support him.
• Chronically lame with medication unable to ease his pain.
• Inoperable tumours, causing chronic pain and impeding the function of limbs or organs.
• Unable to breathe without coughing.
• Crying helplessly, with a worn-out, pleading look, to stop the pain and misery he is going through.

More than likely throughout his long and happy life with you, he will never have experienced anything unpleasant, certainly not discomfort or unbearable pain.

You must be very brave, for he has loved you faithfully every day of his life and now, in his time of need, you are the only one who can help relieve him from further suffering.

When the day comes, you must put your emotions aside. Face up to your duty and send for the vet to come to your home and put your dear old friend peacefully to sleep in his home surroundings. This is so much better than taking him on a final, uncomfortable car journey to the vet's busy surgery.

At home, in his own comfy dog bed, he is resting, quiet and relaxed, under no stress. The vet will greet him kindly and will probably receive a heart-wrenching, trusty wag, which makes the situation even harder to bear. I kneel down and gently stroke my dear Lab's lovely face, give his ears a final gentle caress, and tell him all is well and what a good dog he is. Although inwardly I am torn apart with grief, I must not allow myself to appear distressed, otherwise he will be alarmed. I want his passing to be calm and peaceful.

The vet gently shaves a patch of leg-hair. The final injection is quietly and painlessly given; the deed is done, kindly and quickly with no stress. Within just a few seconds my dear old pal is fast asleep; gone forever, but free at last from pain and discomfort. I am in pieces and am allowed to show it!

Just like me, when you have to say a final goodbye to your dear old Labrador, you and your family will cry your hearts out and grieve for many days. This is quite normal, but always remember that your selfless gift has freed him from further pain.

If wished, your vet will arrange your dog's cremation at a pet crematorium. A few days later, his ashes will be tastefully returned to you in an urn, to be buried in the garden where he played so happily throughout his life.

You will never forget your Labrador and swear you will never replace him. With the passing of time, you may find the gap left in your life without a Labrador too much to bear and eventually, one day, another bright, smiley Labrador puppy will come merrily bouncing through the doorway, to join your family and creep into your heart once again.

The fond memories of your faithful friend will never fade and the joy of watching the antics of the newcomer will surely bring happy memories of the past to the fore, as the cycle of life continues.

In time you will be able to look back and enjoy the happy memories of shared companionship.

"Grieve not, nor speak of me with tears, but laugh and talk of me as if I were beside you... I loved you so – 'twas Heaven here with you."
Isla Paschal Richardson.

Educating Your Labrador

L abradors are very intelligent and are one of the easiest breeds to train. I find the blacks are very bright and are the quickest to learn, with the other two colours not far behind. They are all assisted by their will to please, their great love of food, and the hope of a tasty reward for getting things right.

The short period between eight and twelve weeks of age is very important from a socialisation point of view. Make sure your puppy meets plenty of children and adults while he is young. Once inoculated, I take my puppies in the car to the local supermarket carpark, where they are soon spotted by members of the public, who crowd around the car; the pups are patted and greatly admired, all of which they lap up.

Training sessions should be kept short and interesting in the early days; 10- to 15-minute lessons are sufficient each day, otherwise your pup will get bored. Training should be fun, so never train when your puppy is tired or when you are feeling out of sorts or grumpy!

I use small chunks of cheddar cheese as bait at the puppy age, later switching to soft meaty chews or a tiny biscuit.

TONE OF VOICE

In training, the tone of your voice is essential; use a low, sharp and gruff voice for "bad dog" occurrences; bright, happy and cheery for "good dog" behaviour.

I can recall my mother accusing me of not using the correct tone of voice with some of my early Labradors. She was a Labrador breeder and Championship show judge in the Toy and Utility groups, whose show Labradors in the 1940s and early 1950s were all gun trained and extremely well behaved. I adored my dogs utterly, but, while they were extremely happy, they were probably not the best behaved!

One day she firmly let me know her opinion: "Those dogs think you are a great big joke! Use your voice correctly and they will learn to respect you." She was right! A change in the tone of my voice quickly brought about a change for the better in their manners.

A puppy will soak up new experiences like a sponge.

FIRST LESSONS

A Labrador puppy's brain is like a blank canvas. It pays to commence training from the very first moment he comes to live with you at two months of age. At this time, more than any other, the blank canvas is far more easily filled.

The first thing you will teach him is his chosen name. Each time you talk to him or give him an instruction, preface it with his name to get his attention. Let's call the pup 'Dougal'. On his first day, having just arrived home with him, you will want him to go outside in the garden to the toilet. Get his attention by brightly calling, "Dougal, come", perhaps clapping

your hands as you walk outside. He will happily follow you, since you are the only person he knows in his whole new world.

Once at the correct toilet spot, give the command "Dougal, hurry up", which are the words you will use to train him to go to the toilet. If he gets it right, praise him immediately in a happy cheery voice: "Dougal, good boy, what a clever boy!"

It will be time to go indoors and to give him his first meal. "Dougal, come – dinner" you cheerily call while clapping your hands above his crate. He will arrive at his crate and spy the lovely bowl of food you have put in there for him to eat. His thoughts? "Great crate. Nice dry place, with food provided."

So in just a few minutes, he has made a start to learning his name and the words 'Come', 'Hurry up', 'Good boy', 'Clever boy', and the magical word 'Dinner'. He has also been into his crate for the first time where he found the world's best training aid awaiting – food. From now on, he will always think of his crate as a good place to be. His very own indoor house.

At times when you cannot supervise him, he will be shut in his crate, otherwise leave the door open so he can wander in and out at leisure, possibly lying down in there

A puppy has to find out what is acceptable behaviour.

for a snooze during the day. Whenever you want him to be shut in his crate, get his attention and call his name, saying, "In your house", while you drop a biscuit through the crate's top wire surface. As he sees the biscuit land on his fleece bed, the pup will quickly rush into the crate and you can close the door behind him while he eats the treat. I suggest, during his puppy months, you feed all his meals in the crate, too.

With time he will quickly learn many more words. His doggy vocabulary will eventually include such words as: Wait, Off, Leave, Sit, Stand, Down, Turn, Outside, Get back, Quiet, Bed, and Come out, which is the command to get him out of the dishwasher, when he is much older and taking advantage! Remember, every time you speak to him, call him or give him an instruction, preface the command with his name, as our example, "Dougal", and he will soon become Dougal in his own mind, too. You will use his name before every instruction you give him, throughout his life.

In the early days, he has to find out what is acceptable behaviour in your household and what is not. He will try everything out: tearing up the newspaper, chasing the cat, jumping up your clean trousers with muddy paws, pulling at the tablecloth, chewing your fingers with his sharp baby teeth, carting his food bowl around, sploshing in the water bowl, and digging up the lawn.

All of these no-go exploits will elicit a nasty, sharp, gruff tone of voice from you when you admonish: "Dougal, No! Bad dog." He will stop in his tracks, shocked that his lovely, newfound friend has used such a nasty-sounding, stern voice.

Thus, he concludes, he had better abandon that particular unpopular project and find something else to amuse himself, like playing with a ball or the empty plastic bottle you have given him (with the top removed), until the next meal. Remember, as soon as he is doing something right, praise him. You are the one to teach him the house rules and your tone of voice is the key to success.

No jumping up
Command "OFF"

At the eight-week stage, after his long night's sleep, he will be so happy to see you for the first time in the morning that he will want to jump up to say "Hello" to you before going outside. While jumping up appears very friendly and endearing in a tiny puppy, it is a very bad habit and not appreciated when your energetic Labrador is full-sized, especially on a wet, muddy day. Your Labrador puppy should be taught not to jump up.

To get your puppy used to remaining on all four feet when he

A puppy cannot resist an enthusiastic greeting – but jumping up is a serious problem when a Labrador is fully grown.

sees you first thing in the morning, try dropping a few biscuit treats on the floor for him to search out and eat. He will forget about jumping up and, instead, each morning will anticipate the dropped treats. He will start searching the floor for them as soon as he sees you. Once the treats have been found and eaten, he will then be ready to dash outside as fast as his dumpy little legs will carry him, to his toilet place in the garden. When he has performed in the correct location, more lovely praise and a friendly pat will be forthcoming: "What a good, clever boy!"

When he returns indoors it will be breakfast time, and, once again, if he jumps up, take a few pieces of his breakfast out of his dish and drop them on the floor for him to find while you put the dish down. Should he persist in jumping up, say in a sharp gruff voice: "No, off". We use the command "Off" rather than the command "Down", as the latter will be used when his training is more advanced and you wish him to lie flat on the floor.

First retrieves

Your puppy grows up so quickly. When he is not resting you should make time to enjoy playing with him,

The trick is to train as you play, so your puppy is happy to co-operate.

as this delightful puppy age is soon gone. I play with my pups and start to train them in the kitchen, but anywhere undercover is good. I sit or kneel on the floor, and, as I play with him with a ball or a squeaky toy, I chatter away to him, so he is learning to recognise my voice, as well as hearing and absorbing new words.

Fetch and Come

As our game continues, I gently throw his squeaky toy just a few feet away. His Labrador retrieving instinct tells him to fetch, bring the toy back, and give it to me so that I can throw

it once more. He loves the game. I say: "Fetch" and he scampers off to pick up the toy and return it to me. As soon as he has it in his mouth and turns to come back to me, I encourage him, saying, "Come", which he does, proudly carrying his little toy. "Good boy!" He gets lots of praise.

Sit and Wait

Now is the time to teach him the word "Sit". As he brings back his toy to give it to me, he looks up at me. As he reaches up for the toy, he will lower his hindquarters, and I apply

You can teach the Sit using a treat, a toy, or giving a bowl of food at mealtimes.

hours on end without stopping. Your puppy's gentle retrieving games will have to be very shortlived, just a few minutes only. However, the words Fetch, Come, Sit and Wait will take on meaning. In his doggy mind they will be good happy words, because they are part of a jolly retrieving game. Slowly, bit by bit, his vocabulary and understanding will increase.

Over the next few weeks, he will also be taught good manners, which include walking correctly on the lead and responding outdoors to basic commands. His first lesson will be to wear a collar and to walk on the lead without pulling.

gentle pressure on his rear to get him to sit. I then give the verbal cue "Sit" and reward him. The next time I throw the toy, before he charges off, I tell him to "Wait". I hold him as he watches the toy land and come to a standstill. Then I say "Fetch" and off he goes once again. Another retrieve and another word learnt.

I suggest you also teach your puppy to "Sit" before you put his food dish on the ground at mealtimes, which will reinforce the exercise most effectively.

Adult Labradors will retrieve for

WEARING A COLLAR
When you first bring your puppy home and have got to know each other, while playing with him on the kitchen floor, get him used to wearing a soft puppy collar for a few minutes. Fit the collar gently so that you can get at least two fingers between the

collar and his neck. Initially, he will carry on playing, not noticing that he is wearing the collar. Then, after a while, he will stop, put his back leg up behind his neck and scratch away at the peculiar itchy thing round his neck, which feels so odd.

Bend down, rotate the collar, pat him on the head and distract him by gently throwing a toy for him to retrieve. Once he has worn the collar for a few minutes each day, he will soon ignore it and become used to it.

Remember, never leave the collar on the puppy unsupervised, especially when he is outside in the garden.

WALKING ON THE LEAD

Remember, all commands are prefaced by your puppy's name.

Once your puppy is used to the collar, take him outside into your secure garden where there are no distractions or loose animals; he needs to concentrate. Attach the lead to his collar and teach him to walk to heel beside you on your left-hand side. It is useful to have a wall on your left-hand side so the puppy is sandwiched between you and the wall. This encourages him to walk in a straight line. If there is no wall then use an imaginary straight line.

Give the command "Heel", and, with a tiny jerk on the lead, walk forward, starting with your left leg. Encourage the puppy to walk on your

Most puppies soon adapt to wearing a collar.

left-hand side while you hold the lead in your right hand. Your left hand will be used to restrain the lead should the pup go ahead incorrectly. I find most trusting Labrador puppies will move off happily beside me, but very occasionally one will not. He either stops dead in his tracks, or leaps about like a bucking bronco. If a puppy does this, I quietly ignore him.

The aim is for your Labrador to walk on a loose lead, neither pulling ahead nor lagging behind.

I repeat the command "Heel" with his name, and, looking forwards and not directly at him, with a gentle tug of the lead, I prepare to walk off again. Always remember: look ahead, not at the puppy.

If your puppy is happy to set off and walk beside you, give lots of praise and encouragement, but if he puts the brakes on once again, try enticing him forward with a piece of cheese or tiny biscuit treat – something never known to fail with a Labrador. Within a few days, he will be walking happily on the lead and will never look back.

WALKING TO HEEL

Having got him used to the soft puppy collar and lead, he now needs to learn the art of walking to heel and not pulling like a train or lagging behind sniffing everything he comes across. When teaching this lesson with a puppy, I still use a puppy collar and lead.

This is where training in the confined space beside a wall is useful. If the dog pulls ahead of you, firmly say, "No. Heel." Stop, stand still, and, gently but firmly, bring him back to your left heel. Once back in position, praise him and then set off

Training Tip Reminders

- Never train if you feel in a bad mood or are preoccupied.
- Train puppies for 10-15 minutes only.
- Training should be fun not boring.
- Preface each command with your puppy's name.
- Teach only one lesson at a time and only proceed to the next lesson when the first has been mastered.
- Praise success lavishly and ignore failure.

again, using his name with the word "Heel". Each time he pulls ahead, bring him back to heel. When he finally gets it right, make sure you tell him what a good puppy he is. Cease the lesson on that particular high point, and enjoy a few minutes of relaxed playtime with some toys.

STAY

The ability to obey the command "Stay" could mean the difference between life or death for your Labrador.

Consider this personal experience of mine. One day, several years ago, before I lived in the countryside, I crossed a busy main road with my Labrador walking on the lead, quietly at heel. Out of the blue, right under our noses, a squirrel burst forth from the hedgerow bottom. It excitedly darted over the road, and, as I watched it, with horror I also noted a red double-decker bus fast approaching at speed, on our side of the road.

The excitement of the squirrel's sudden appearance passed to my Labrador, who somehow slipped his lead. His immediate thought was to chase the squirrel, which had suddenly appeared at his feet and then shot across the road. In a flash, he too was off across the road. He charged after the squirrel, which then stopped in its tracks on the opposite pavement. Having seen the speeding dog careering towards it, the squirrel then decided to double

A reliable response to the "Stay" could be a lifesaver.

Teach your puppy to 'Sit" and "Stay" so you can leave him at some distance.

back across the road, regardless of the approaching bus, and, once accomplished, disappeared into the hedge bottom from whence it came.

I was frightened and horrified. My dog was still on the far side of the road, and the bus, full of passengers, was almost upon us. I had to stop him charging in front of it to get back to the squirrel. My dog was likely to be killed or cause a frightful accident. I shouted at the excited dog in the best commanding voice I have ever mustered: "No! Stay!" with my hand held up in the commanding "Stay" position, and, miraculously, he did stay – right there on the other side of the road as the bus sailed by with its load of passengers blissfully unaware of the drama! To this day I praise the heavens that I taught him the simple command and hand signal "Stay" when he was a puppy.

Teaching Stay

- Tell your puppy to "Sit" facing you, with the lead loose in your left hand, attached to his collar.
- Take a step backwards and raise your right hand, like a policeman. Give the command "Stay" and take another step backwards.
- If he moves or tries to wander off, quietly correct him – "No. Stay" – and put him back in position.
- Repeat the exercise until he gets it right. Then make it more interesting. Give the command "Stay", move backwards or out to either side of your puppy. If he stays correctly, walk back to him and praise him. Eventually, try

walking in a circle around him. He will learn to watch you and "Stay", without moving, wherever you are. Give him lots of praise, in a happy tone.

- Once you think he is steady, try the lesson without the lead.

"COME": OUTDOORS

When your puppy is capable of walking to heel, sitting and staying, teach the recall – "Come" – which he may have already learnt to do in the confined space of your kitchen, but not in the wide open space of outdoors.

Take him outside into the garden. Attach a long extending lead or washing line to his collar, place the pup in the "Sit" position, and walk to the end of the lead or rope. Turn around. Reinforce the "Sit" and "Stay" with your verbal command and raised right hand, palm towards the dog.

Make sure you sound bright and inviting as you give the command 'Come".

Give lots of praise when your puppy reaches you.

other dogs around and without the rope. This can be practised at group training classes. The Kennel Club will advise of your nearest class.

If your dog does run off and he ignores you, you must *not* scold him when he finally does return. He has returned – admittedly rather later than expected – but you want him to associate coming back to you as a pleasant thing, not for a telling off.

Should he continue to run off, you need to go right back to the very beginning of his recall training and start all over again on the lead.

When you are ready, call his name brightly, and, tapping your knees rapidly and enthusiastically, prefaced by his name, call: "Come". You can also use a training whistle to do this, making several toots to which he will learn to respond.

Your puppy will probably set off at great speed and cannon himself towards you. As he arrives, in the last few strides give the command "Sit", with right hand raised again. Praise him lavishly when he comes to a halt, seated in front of your legs and facing you.

Gradually, increase the distance at which you perform this exercise. Eventually, aim to do the recall with

"DOWN" or "FLAT"

These are the commands to get your dog lying flat on the floor and can be taught indoors or out. Either word may be used.

With your dog on the lead and in the Sit position on your left-hand side, kneel down with your knee on the end of his lead so he cannot run off. Show your dog you are holding a treat in your right hand. Then, close your fist around the treat and move your hand towards the floor

Your puppy will follow the treat as you lower it towards the ground and go into the Down position.

between your dog's front legs, giving the command "Down". He is, after all, a typical, hungry Labrador so, obviously, his nose will follow the treat in your hand down to the floor. Gradually move the treat forward and his body will be horizontal in the Down position. Give him the treat and praise him. Repeat the exercise frequently. Gradually, as he learns this command, you can perfect the straightness of his position.

Labradors learn so quickly and love pleasing you. You will be thrilled and impressed with the results of your training skills.

NEW CHALLENGES

If you are enjoying training your Labrador, you may want to get involved in more advanced training, or take part in one of the many canine sports on offer.

Good Citizen Scheme

If you are not proposing to show your puppy, enrol in the Good Citizen Scheme, which offers the best training classes for pet dogs. Again, you can obtain the address of your nearest class from the Kennel Club.

The Good Citizen Scheme was devised by the Kennel Club to teach basic obedience. The prized Bronze, Silver and Gold Good Citizen awards are the goals to aim for with your Labrador. You will make many friends at the classes and enjoy training your own dog in a group of like-minded people, and you will also have the pleasure of owning a beautifully behaved Labrador.

Ringcraft

If you intend to show your puppy, you will need to attend these classes from when he is four months old. The Kennel Club will advise of your nearest class.

At ringcraft classes he will meet lots of different breeds of dogs, which he has never seen before: Pugs that look at him with goggly eyes and snuffle loudly, strutting Poodles with fancy hair-styles and boisterous terriers who never stop yapping. He will be taught all aspects of the show ring: how to stand correctly, to be examined by the judge and have his teeth inspected, and to move correctly at the right pace, up and down a mat. He will also learn how to socialise with the other dogs at the class.

Get your pup immunised against kennel cough before his first class, otherwise he is likely to pick up this contagious cough, to which young Labs seem susceptible. If he does pick up kennel cough, he will be unable to go to classes for a month or more, which will delay his education at an important time.

If you have a good specimen of the breed, you may decide to get involved in showing your Labrador.

Dog shows

When your Labrador has learnt how to behave in the ring, you are ready to compete. The first classes are for puppies from six months of age and progress through different categories. There are different types of shows you can attend:

Companion shows are enter-on-the-day, light-hearted events with Pedigree classes for pedigree dogs and Novelty classes, open to all dogs.

Open shows and Championship shows are for KC registered dogs only in breed-specific classes, judged on conformation to the Breed Standard. These shows are entered several weeks beforehand and are judged by Kennel Club approved judges.

Showing is great fun, but at the top level it is highly competitive, so you will need to learn the art of winning – and losing – gracefully.

Agility

This is great fun to watch and join in. Against the clock, at the fastest speed they can muster, dogs jump over obstacles, through tyres and tunnels, and negotiate the contact equipment, which includes an A frame, a dog walk and a seesaw.

While the Labrador will enjoy agility, he is not the speediest. However, with training, he will become a reliable competitor and you will both get a lot of fun from taking part.

Agility is fun sport for both dog and handler.

Obedience

If your Labrador has mastered basic obedience, you may want to get involved in competitive obedience. The exercises include: heelwork at varying paces with dog and handler following a pattern decided by the judge, stays, recalls, retrieves, sendaways, scent discrimination and distance control. The exercises get progressively harder as you progress up the classes.

A Labrador will readily learn the exercises that are used in obedience competitions, but, at the top level, a very high degree of precision and accuracy is called for.

Working training and working tests

Local Gundog Clubs hold working training classes, which are greatly enjoyed during the summer. You will meet many new friends while bringing out your Labrador's working ability, be he show or working-bred.

Labradors are trained to move in line off the lead at heel; to sit steadily and quietly in line with other dogs; to sit and be steady when there is gunshot; to watch and mark dummies that have been thrown forwards, backwards or sideways on land and in water, and, when asked, to retrieve those dummies straight back to hand.

Novice working tests, held under Kennel Club rules, test your dog's working ability after training. More advanced training leads to intermediate and working tests, using dead game instead of dummies. Eventually, during the shooting season, you may be invited to go "picking up" with your well-trained Labrador on a local shoot.

Field trials

These are highly competitive, sometimes arduous, events over rough territory, held under Kennel Club rules to resemble a day's shooting in the field. Field trial

Labradors will be from a working background as opposed to showing, and are expected to work with all manner of game, from rabbits and hares, to partridges and pheasants.

The Young Kennel Club

The Young Kennel Club is a great organisation for any child who loves dogs. There are three age categories of membership for children and young adults.

Young members are taught responsible dog ownership. They can take the family's Labrador and join in training classes, covering many topics, including show handling, agility, obedience, flyball, and heelwork to music. In the summer holidays there is an annual summer camp, and each week at shows around the country there are YKC classes to compete in.

SUMMING UP

You may have ambitions to compete at a low level or you may have ambitions to reach the very top, but whatever you choose to do, owning a well-behaved Labrador will bring you and your family much credit and enjoyment for many years.

If you work your Labrador, you will have to build up a special rapport so your dog has the motivation to learn new exercises.

Health Care For Labradors

Once you have decided on your veterinary practice, it is important to take your new Labrador for a health-check as soon as possible. This first examination can be the beginning of a long and happy relationship between your Labrador and his veterinary surgeon, and it is a good idea for your vet to get to know him from an early age.

Regular 'weigh-ins' and visits to the surgery to pick up medication for worming and treatment of fleas will accustom him to visiting the vet with no adverse experiences. A few dog treats go a long way in making the consulting room a pleasant place! It is also a good idea for you to mimic a clinical examination at home so your Labrador is used to having his ears, eyes, mouth and body inspected.

VACCINATION

Vaccination is vital to prevent and control some of the severe viral and bacterial diseases that can be fatal to dogs. Vaccines work by stimulating the body's natural immune response to provide protection should your dog ever be exposed to the disease. This protection is continued each year by annual booster vaccinations. It is important to remember that your Labrador should be as fit and healthy as possible to help the vaccine work fully.

Puppies obtain antibodies from their mother's colostrum (first milk) providing immunity to disease for the first few weeks of life. The level of immunity depends on antibodies absorbed from the colostrum and how well the mother is protected from certain diseases. Over a period of time, differing for each puppy, these antibodies decrease, and, from six weeks of age, a puppy will need his first vaccination. The initial vaccination course contains at least two injections, the second vaccination being after 10 weeks of age. Contact with unvaccinated dogs or at-risk areas should be avoided until full immunity is established.

Microchipping can be carried out at the same time. This is where a microchip, an electronic chip roughly

A vaccination programme should be started when a puppy is around eight weeks of age.

the size of a grain of rice, is inserted under the skin. This ensures that your dog is traceable and the microchipping company can contact you should your Lab ever accidentally become separated from you.

The diseases protected against by standard vaccination protocols are briefly outlined here, but if your Labrador is diagnosed with any of the following, he should be kept away from other dogs to prevent the spread of infection.

- **Distemper:** Caused by the canine distemper virus (CDV)
- **Infectious canine hepatitis:** Caused by canine adenovirus-1 (CAV-1)
- **Parvovirus:** Caused by canine parvovirus (CPV) that can survive for months to years in the environment
- **Leptospirosis:** Often carried by rats and caused by two main strains of spirochaete bacteria, *Lepstospira icterohaemorrhagiae* (affecting the liver) and *L. canicola* (affecting the kidneys)
- **Kennel cough:** Caused by multiple viral and bacterial agents, resulting in a harsh cough that may be very severe, especially in the very young and old. Labradors appear to be prone to infection with kennel cough so it is important to include this in your annual vaccination routine
- **Herpes:** Caused by the canine herpes virus (CHV)

PARASITES

Labradors are outgoing and active working dogs with an interest – and a nose – in everything! This will result in contact with parasites, both internal and external, but is not necessarily a serious issue if they are adequately controlled. There are several types of worms, the most common being the roundworm. Most puppies are born infected with roundworms and infection in adults often occurs from eating infected faeces or meat or via an intermediate host.

In most cases treatment requires worming medication to remove the infection and ongoing preventative medication to prevent build-up. All worming medication should be discussed with your veterinary surgeon (with regard to timing, frequency and preparation). There may be some indication that in Labrador puppies worming medication should be given a few days after vaccination, as they may become poorly if given on the same day.

Strict hygiene, especially with faeces, should always be observed. When out walking your dog, faeces should be removed from public places with a bag, and many parks now provide disposal bins specifically for this purpose. This, as well as enabling walking without stepping into things you would rather not, helps reduce infection of other dogs and, in some cases, humans.

Roundworm

- *Toxocara cani:* This is a large, round, white worm found in the small intestine. Signs of infection are a pot-belly, occasional diarrhoea or vomiting, poor growth, lethargy, coughing, pneumonia, nasal discharge and even death in young pups with very heavy infections. Regular worming of pups and mother during the early periods of the puppies' lives will prevent severe infections. Adult dogs should be treated every three to six months throughout their lives. It is important to note that, although unlikely, this worm can infect humans, particularly children who have had close contact with household pets or areas contaminated with dog faeces, potentially resulting in liver damage or blindness.
- *Toxascaris leonina:* Infection occurs via direct ingestion of the egg or as larvae in the tissues of mice and are almost always concurrent with *T. canis* therefore clinical signs and treatment regimes are similar.

Whipworms

- *Trichuris vulpis:* Whipworms have a thick tail and a thin head, hence the name. Light infections often cause no signs, but if heavy burdens are present, watery diarrhoea may be seen, often with blood and mucus present.

Puppies should be routinely wormed for roundworm.

Tapeworm

- *Dipylidium caninum:* This is the most common of the tapeworm species in the UK. Infection occurs via ingestion of fleas and lice carrying the intermediate lifestage of the worm. The adult worms live in the small intestine and release proglottids (mobile segments containing the eggs) into the faeces. The adults rarely cause clinical disease, although irritation of the anus may be seen as the proglottids emerge. Treatment and control are integral, with insecticide treatment preventing the completion of the lifecycle, while regular worming medication removes the adult worms.

Lungworm

- *Angiostrongylus vasorum:*
  Commonly known as lungworm, this parasite lives in the heart and lungs of dogs and foxes and can cause serious illness and even death in affected animals. Once rare in the UK, it is becoming more common, particularly in the south of England. The parasite is transmitted from dog and fox faeces to slugs and snails. Dogs are then infected by eating infected slugs and snails. Labradors may try to eat slugs and snails given the opportunity, especially when younger, so it is important always to supervise your dog when outside and be aware of the symptoms of lungworm infection (such as a persistent cough and breathing difficulties). Ask your vet's advice on the most suitable wormer for your Labrador if you know he is a snail eater (not all worming preparations are effective against lungworm).

Fleas

- *Ctenocephalides canis* and *C. felis* (more common): The flea is a small, wingless insect with a laterally flattened body and biting mouthparts enabling it to feed on blood. Adults live on the host, and

- **Taenia species** *(T. multiceps, T. hydatigena, T. ovis, T. pisiformis, T. serialis):* Infection occurs via ingestion of infected meat of the intermediate hosts (sheep, rabbits, rodents). These worms are often not of clinical significance in the dog, but are far more important in the intermediate hosts where they can be fatal. Prevention of access to infected meat and regular worming medication controls infection.

- **Echinococcus granulosus:** *This tapeworm is found in the small intestine in* dogs, and as larvae in the liver or lungs of the intermediate host (ruminants, man or pig). Large infections are often no issue in the dog. If man is the intermediate host, this may be more severe with clinical signs relating to the larvae forming potentially fatal cysts in the lungs or liver.

the resulting hundreds of eggs, larvae and pupae are found in the environment. Both species are part of the lifecycle of the common tapeworm of dogs *D. caninum*. When the flea bites, it causes irritation to the skin, which results in pruritis (itching) and inflammation. Regular flea insecticide treatment is required on the dog and good hygiene and aerosol treatment in the environment to help break the reproductive cycle and reduce numbers. Labradors can suffer allergic reactions to the saliva of the fleas, which may require further medication, such as antibiotics

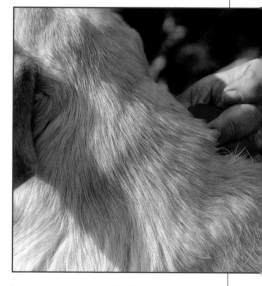

Spot on treatment is effective in preventing infestation from fleas.

Ticks

The common types of tick found on dogs in the UK are the *Ixodes ricinus* (sheep tick, also found on deer) and the *I. hexagonus* (hedgehog tick). They are blood-sucking parasites that can transmit diseases, such as Lyme disease (to both dogs and humans) and Ehrlichiosis. Bean shaped, they vary in size from 2-10mm and are most commonly found on dogs in spring and autumn. As they feed they swell in size and heavy infestations can cause anaemia. Once the female has mated, she feeds and then drops off the host to lay thousands of eggs. Ticks can be removed using a tick removal tool by engaging the hook under the tick and flat to the skin of the dog, and twisting the body until the tick comes out. Take care not to squeeze the body or leave the mouthparts in the skin, as infection can occur.

Ticks are a growing problem in the UK.

Ringworm/ Dermatophytosis

Microsporum canis is responsible for the majority of ringworm cases with *Trichophyton mentagrophytes* and *Microsporum gypseum* also seen. Typically, circular lesions are present with skin scaling and hair loss noted. Topical treatment is used and if infection is severe antibiotics may also be needed.

and/or steroids in conjunction with insecticidal medication.

Lice

Lice are highly host-specific and unable to survive for long when off the host body. Dogs are hosts to two types of louse, *Linognathus* and *Trichodectes* (a carrier of the tapeworm *D. caninum*). Infection results in irritation and skin damage and severe infestations may cause anaemia. Prescription shampoo is often suitable to eliminate infection.

Mites

• **Otodectes cyanotic:** This mite is found in the external ear canal and causes the production of a brown, waxy discharge, resulting in head shaking, discomfort and pruritis. It can be transmitted by close contact. Infection can be cleared by cleaning the ear canal and applying medicated drops, but, if left untreated, secondary infection may occur. This can cause ear drum rupture, resulting in deafness and neurological signs, and may prove difficult to treat.

• **Cheyletiella yasguri:** This mite is visible with the naked eye and is often referred to as 'walking dandruff'. It is a non-burrowing mite that causes pruritis, scaling and scabs on the skin. Treatment is available and effective. Care must be taken, as this parasite is zoonotic (transferable to humans).

• **Demodex canis:** This cigar-shaped burrowing mite is found in small numbers on healthy dogs, but disease can occur if the immune system is compromised. Transmission occurs between mother and pups while feeding, and infection is often seen in young dogs with scaling, hair loss, pustules and skin infections (especially around the face). Occasionally the feet may be affected. Treatment involves repeated applications of topical medication and occasionally antibiotics.

- *Sarcoptes scabiei:* This highly contagious burrowing mite causes intense pruritis around the ears, muzzle, face and elbows and, if severe, all over the body. Clinical signs involve pustules, crust formation, alopecia and there may be self trauma from itching. Treatment requires repeated bathing with a medicated shampoo, with isolation until eliminated to prevent transmission.

Dental Problems

Periodontal disease is the most common oral disease in dogs, and Labradors are no exception. Tartar can be seen as young as nine months of age and is normally first noticed on the upper back teeth, spreading and getting worse over time. Your dog's teeth should be examined regularly to assess the level of disease and decide whether treatment is necessary.

Initially plaque (soft debris, bacteria and staining) deposits on the teeth, which, over time, mineralises and forms tartar. Once tartar is present, it spreads under the gums, causing pain and inflammation (gingivitis) seen as reddening of the gums. The bacteria in the tartar can enter the bloodstream, due to the increased blood supply, which occurs during the inflammatory process, and be carried to the organs (e.g. liver, kidneys), resulting in infection. Severe tartar causes gum recession, root exposure and loss of teeth.

Minimal deposit on the teeth can be controlled with a healthy diet, tooth brushing and dental chews. Tooth brushing should be taught at an early age

A-Z OF COMMON AILMENTS

Anal gland disorders

Anal glands are small sacs that empty into the anus when defecation occurs. They produce a dark-brown, pungent liquid, which is used by dogs to mark their territory.

Occasionally the anal sacs may become blocked or impacted, resulting in irritation. This can cause your Lab to drag his bottom along the floor (known as 'scooting'), or to nibble around the tail area. He may also have problems trying to defecate.

If the anal glands become blocked, they can be manually expressed to clear the blockage. If the blockage is not cleared then infection may occur and form an abscess within the gland. This will need veterinary attention.

Factors that may play a part in causing impaction are diarrhoea, soft faeces and obesity. Labradors, especially if overweight, seem to be prone to anal gland problems and

– prevention is better than cure! Once tartar has formed, this cannot be removed by brushing and will only become worse with time. At this point, an anaesthetic may be needed to remove the tartar manually. The condition of the teeth beneath the tartar determines whether or not they need extracting. After dentistry, it is very important to maintain dental health and it may be advisable to alter the diet to encompass your dog's dental requirements.

The aim is to keep the teeth clean and the gums healthy.

The Labrador's love of water makes him susceptible to ear infections.

adding a little bran to their diet to firm the faeces may help. In some cases persistent recurrence may require surgery to remove the gland completely.

Ear infections

The ear is made up of three sections:

- **The external ear:** This includes the pinna (earflap) and the ear canal extending as far as the tympanic membrane (ear drum).
- **The middle ear:** This is an air-filled cavity that contains three small bones that vibrate and transmit the sound to the inner ear.
- **The inner ear:** This is a fluid-filled cavity that contains the cochlea (organ for hearing) and the vestibular apparatus (organ involved in balance).

Infection can occur commonly in the outer ear (otitis externa), resulting in a brown, waxy discharge, often accompanied with a characteristic smell and reddening of the skin. This will cause your dog to shake his head or scratch at his ears in response to the irritation. If the

Foreign bodies, such as grass seeds, may be responsible for ear infections.

infection spreads deeper into the middle ear (otitis media) or inner ear (otitis interna) then this may cause neurological signs, such as lack of co-ordination, imbalance, circling or a head tilt.

Labradors tend to be very susceptible to ear infections and irritations due to their narrow ear canals and love of water. Occasionally foreign bodies (e.g. grass seeds) can enter the ear canal and remain there. Ear mites (see page 101) cause irritation and wax production. Bacteria and yeasts can enter the ear and infection occurs when their growth becomes uncontrolled. Allergic skin disease can be common in the Labrador and usually manifests as itching, but occasionally the only sign seen may be ear disorders.

Treatment involves clearing any infection and removing excess wax. There are many topical preparations available, but if infection is severe or non-responsive, investigation under anaesthetic may be required to flush the ear canal. If left untreated, the ear may become impacted, the skin

Endocrine Disorders

- **Diabetes mellitus (DM):** This is one of the more common endocrine disorders encountered, most often seen in middle-aged, overweight dogs with the older, entire female Labrador being predisposed. Glucose is absorbed by cells in the presence of insulin, and is the energy source for cell survival.

  DM occurs when insulin production (by the pancreas) is inadequate or the body's cells fail to respond to insulin properly. This results in an inability to absorb the glucose, causing high blood levels and subsequently glucose in the urine. The most common clinical signs are excessive drinking and urination, increased appetite and weight loss, although coat changes and lethargy may also occur. If left untreated, it can progress to blindness caused by cataracts or further to a diabetic coma. Treatment is comparable to humans with daily insulin injections for life.

- **Hyperadrenocorticism (Cushing's disease):** This is where there is excessive production of cortisol hormone from the adrenal glands, often seen in older, larger breed dogs and the older, female Labrador may be at a slightly

may become thickened from chronic inflammation and ultimately surgery may be the only option.

Eye disorders

- **Eyelids:** The eyelids cover and protect the delicate structures of the eye and ensure that the outer surface remains clean and lubricated. Labradors can suffer from entropion (inward rotation) of the eyelids, which may cause inflammation and infection. They may also get small, wart-like growths on the lids, which is not a problem unless they grow large or touch the cornea, causing trauma.
- **Lens:** The lens is found behind the pupil and focuses light rays so that objects can be seen clearly.

higher risk. This can be caused directly by tumours of the adrenal glands or tumours in the brain, resulting in overstimulation of the adrenal glands. Clinical signs are excessive drinking and urination, increased appetite, weakness, hair loss and often a pot-bellied appearance. Treatment involves lifelong oral medication and occasionally surgery to remove the tumour if possible.

- **Hypothyroidism:** This is where there is underproduction of thyroxine (hormone controlling metabolic rate of the body) from the thyroid gland. Generally seen in middle-aged dogs of larger breeds and it can be occasionally seen in Labradors. The low levels result in weakness, lethargy, reduced body temperature, weight gain, slow heart rate, hair loss, and skin problems. Treatment, often successful, is in the form of an oral synthetic hormone.

- **Hypoadrenocorticism (Addison's disease):** This is a less common disease where there is reduced production of mineralocorticoids and glucocorticoids from the adrenal glands. Clinical signs are vomiting, diarrhoea, weight loss, weakness and an abnormally slow heart rate. Treatment long term is often successful and involves giving the deficient hormones in tablet form for life.

Cataracts (See Hereditary Disorders) are an opacification (blue-whitening) of the lens, progressively resulting in impaired vision, not to be confused with nuclear sclerosis (grey-blue haze), which occurs in older animals and doesn't cause blindness.

- **Retina:** The retina is the layer at the back of the eye that receives light rays and is composed of cells called rods and cones. Rods aid vision in low light and cones help determine different colours; a dog's eyes are especially plentiful in rods compared to humans hence better in lower light levels but not in colour. See Hereditary Disorders for more information on retinal problems in the Labrador.

The eyes should be bright and sparkling, with no hint of soreness, inflammation or discharge.

- **Cornea:** The cornea is the transparent layer at the front of the eye that allows light to enter. With their need to investigate every bit of undergrowth, Labradors may occasionally damage the cornea. Trauma to the cornea can result in tear production, blinking and pain, and, if untreated, may progress to infection and ulceration. Ulceration is where some of the cornea is damaged, often accompanied by conjunctivitis. If superficial then this may be treated with medicated eye drops, but if the injury persists or the initial ulcer is deeper, then there is a risk of rupture of the eye. Conjunctivitis is the term for inflammation, discomfort and reddening of the conjunctiva (tissues around the eye). There are many causes of conjunctivitis from bacterial and viral to trauma. Any sign of conjunctivitis could potentially be serious and requires veterinary attention.

Gastrointestinal disorders

• **Foreign bodies:** All dogs like to play with toys (and what they think are their toys but in fact are the family heirloom!) and to feel the sensation of new substances with their mouths. Labradors also seem to enjoy swallowing them, which may result in the intestine becoming either partially or completely obstructed. Complete obstruction in the oesophagus will result in choking and an inability to breathe whereas a partial blockage will allow breathing to occur but may cause discomfort or pain.

Blockages further down the intestinal tract can result in anorexia, vomiting, abdominal pain or diarrhoea. The degree of severity of clinical signs usually depends on the degree and duration of obstruction. If a blockage has occurred, the only option is surgery to remove the obstruction.

• **Intestinal intussusception:** This is where the intestine folds in on itself, often caused by hypermotility (excessive gut movement), to form a double tube that constricts, causing obstruction. Obstruction may initially be partial and proceed to complete. This condition is more common in young dogs six to eight months, with clinical signs being vomiting, abdominal pain,

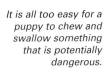

It is all too easy for a puppy to chew and swallow something that is potentially dangerous.

anorexia and diarrhoea, occasionally with blood. Surgery is needed to remove any damaged intestine.

- **Gastritis:** This is inflammation of the stomach lining, typically resulting in vomiting. There are multiple causes, with scavenging high on the list of probabilities and Labradors often have appetites as large and generous as their nature! Vomiting is the body's natural defence against poisoning and occasionally dogs may eat grass to bring on vomiting if they feel nauseous. Single episodes of

Common Causes Of Diarrhoea

There are many reasons for diarrhoea. Often frequency of defecation increases and there may be blood or mucus present. Sometimes 24-hour withdrawal of food can be enough to help clear any upset. At other times the condition can be life-threatening. If your Labrador is unwell or off colour, if he is vomiting, or blood is noted in the faeces, veterinary advice should be sought.

Common causes of diarrhoea include:

- **Dietary:** Any dog owner will know that all dogs at some point eat something that would not normally be considered on a menu! Rubbish bins are often a favourite of Labradors, but may contain unsavoury and potentially poisonous items. Therefore, bins inside and outside the house should be well secured. Sudden diet changes can upset the normal intestinal microflora, so any diet alteration should be carried out over a four- to five-day period, gradually increasing the amount of the new diet. Hypersensitivities to food can be seen in the Labrador (often with concurrent skin problems). resulting in chronic diarrhoea, vomiting are often seen and are not a problem in the dog as long as he remains bright and well. If vomiting continues or your dog appears unwell, a trip to the vet will be needed.

- **Gastric dilatation volvulus (bloat/torsion):** This is where the stomach swells visibly (dilatation) and then rotates (volvulus) so that the exit into the small intestine becomes blocked preventing food from leaving. This results in stomach pain and a bloated abdomen. It is a severe, life-threatening condition that requires and it can be a frustrating condition to diagnose, involving diet trials with specially formulated feedstuffs.

- **Bacterial infections (*Salmonella, Campylobacter, E. coli*):** Care needs to be taken if these have been diagnosed, as they are potentially transmissible to humans, so strict hygiene methods should be employed to minimise the risks. Antibiotics are the mainstay of treatment, but severe cases may need hospitalisation.

- **Viral infections (canine distemper, canine parvovirus, coronavirus):** These often require supportive treatment, as there is rarely antiviral therapy available.

- **Parasites:** A heavy worm burden may result in diarrhoea, and a regular worming regime should be employed to prevent them being a possible cause of any upset.

- **Enteritis:** This is inflammation of the small intestine and again there is a long list of potential causes. Diarrhoea in large volumes with minimal straining occurs and may be seen with abdominal pain, dehydration, vomiting, anorexia and weight loss. Treatment is dependent on the cause, severity and duration of the disease.

- **Colitis:** This is inflammation of the colon and can have multiple causes. Often diarrhoea is seen, which may be watery in consistency with either blood or mucus or both present. Repeated attempts to pass faeces are seen, with straining, often only producing small volumes. Treatment is dependent on the cause, severity and duration of disease.

The Labrador is vulnerable to joint disorders while he is growing.

immediate veterinary attention (usually surgery) to decompress and return the stomach to its normal position. It is usually seen in large deep-chested breeds and there may be some relation to greedy, fast-eating dogs compounded by exercise immediately after eating. Labradors may be particularly susceptible, as they have all the necessary characteristics.

Joint disorders

The bones and joints of all dogs are sensitive to physical trauma and disease, and even with four legs they occasionally manage to lose their footing and trip! Labradors are physically active dogs and enjoy energetic, chase games, which occasionally may result in trauma.

Initial clinical signs that there may be a problem are lameness, stiffness and pain on movement. Usually a full physical examination and X-rays are necessary to help diagnose the problem. Any trauma to a joint will result in an increased susceptibility of that joint to succumb to arthritis later in life.

- **Osteoarthritis (OA):** This degenerative joint disease results in the joints becoming enlarged, painful and stiff. Often seen in the older Labrador, the first signs may be stiffness and slight lameness, especially after longer walks, which progress to a reluctance to exercise and severe lameness. There are many joint supplements and diets available to help slow progression of the disease, and pain-relieving medications to make your dog more comfortable in more severe cases. Ensuring that your Labrador does not put on weight in later years will reduce the load on the joints.
- **Hip dysplasia (HD):** See Inherited Disorders
- **Elbow dysplasia (ED):** See Inherited Disorders
- **Osteochodrosis (OC) and Osteochondritis Dissecans (OCD):** This is where there is inflammation and pain of the bone and cartilage (OC), often due to growth abnormalities or trauma, and the ensuing damage resulting in a flap of cartilage breaking off into the joint (OCD). The young

growing Labrador may be predisposed to this as part of the hereditary elbow dysplasia disorder. It can be a very painful condition, especially if the fragment moves within the joint, and surgery may be indicated to remove it.

- **Cruciate rupture:** The cruciate ligaments of the stifle (knee) can be partially or completely torn when placed under high amounts of physical stress, resulting in lameness. It's more commonly seen in the Labrador, more so if overweight, with young neutered dogs possibly being predisposed. Treatment often involves surgery along with an extended period of rest. The affected joint is prone to arthritis later in life.

Obesity

Physical fitness is a very important aspect of your dog's routine healthcare. Labradors enjoy exercise and will work all day but have a bottomless pit for a stomach! Obesity can have concerning medical effects, and with more dogs nowadays being overweight, a corresponding increase in weight-related medical problems are also being noted.

- A high body-fat percentage increases anaesthetic and surgical risks.
- With increased body weight, there

A healthy diet and regular exercise are the key factors in preventing obesity.

is more physical stress placed on the muscles, bones and joints, and this can result in severe arthritis and joint problems in later life.

- Increased amounts of fat are also deposited around the internal organs, as in humans, and result in reduced function or dysfunction.
- Other medical diseases, such as diabetes, heart disease and breathing problems.

Regular exercise and a healthy diet from the start are the magic ingredients to a fit and healthy dog. Treats can be high in fats and sugars, and should not be given on a regular basis. Using part of the daily diet ration is a good way to treat without increasing the calorific intake. Human food is often unsuitable for dogs and may be poisonous, so take care when giving scraps from your plate. There are specially formulated diets available to help with weight loss, but they need to be used together with increased exercise and a strict 'no treats' regime.

Skin conditions

Labradors should have a thick double coat and healthy skin. There are, however, a few conditions that can affect them.

- **Atopy:** This is an inherited predisposition to develop a hypersensitivity to environmental allergens (e.g. pollens, dust mites, moulds). Initial signs are localised licking, itching and reddening of skin and may progress to generalised self trauma, secondary infection, scaling and crusting. Treatment can involve steroids, antibiotics and even desensitisation vaccines following skin testing to determine the causative allergen.

- **Acral lick dermatitis:** Occasionally Labradors will persistently lick or chew at an area of skin, resulting in trauma. Inciting causes may include trauma, allergies, infection or arthritis. Treatment depends on the causative factor but invariably involves a lot of time and patience to help resolve the problem.
- **Tumours:** Labradors do suffer from some skin tumours as they get

older – commonly lipomas (benign fatty lumps), but they are also predisposed to some malignant tumours. Any lumps or bumps that you notice should be examined by your vet, who may advise taking a sample to be checked by a pathologist to determine treatment.

- **Pyotraumatic dermatitis (hot spot):** This is where the skin becomes infected, often following an insect bite, with oozing and hair loss over the affected area. Topical treatment and daily bathing are often required, with antibiotics if severe.
- **Interdigital cysts/furunculosis:** These are small lumps that occur between the toes, which generally occur as a result of an infection of the hair follicles.

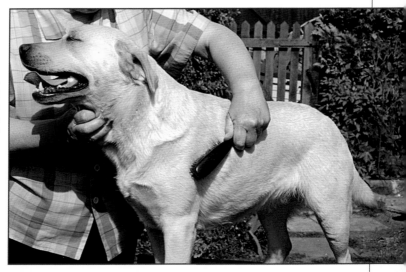

Regular grooming will ensure you keep a close check on your Labrador's skin.

Topical treatment, bathing and antibiotics may be indicated.

- **Naso-digital hyperkeratosis:** This is where the skin of the nose and pads becomes dry and thickened. Treatment is not necessary unless severe.

MISCELLANEOUS

Dead tail

Labradors do suffer from a condition known as 'dead tail', 'cold tail' or 'limber tail'. This is most often seen in working breeds and may have

Urinary Problems

Urine is produced in the kidneys (by filtering blood), transported via the ureters (tubes) to the bladder, where it is stored before being passed through the urethra (a tube) to the penis or vagina and voided. Any abnormality of urine or the act of urination can indicate a problem at any point of the urinary tract. Your Labrador should always have free access to fresh water at all times to help reduce the risk of problems.

Clinical signs are often similar irrespective of the cause. Look for straining or repeated attempts to pass urine; difficult, slow or painful urination; incontinence and abnormally strong smelling or dark-coloured urine. If you notice any of these then, if possible, collect a fresh sample in a clean glass jar and take it with you to the veterinary surgery so they can analyse it after examining your dog.

A few of the common problems are listed below:

- Bacterial cystitis: This is a bacterial infection in the bladder and is more commonly, but not exclusively, seen in bitches. Older, Labrador females appear to be prone and often antibiotics are indicated to help clear the infection.
- Bladder stones (uroliths): These are stones formed within the bladder and although small to start with, may become very large. Factors affecting formation of uroliths are diet, water intake, breed, and

some connection with swimming in cold water (potentially just a bath) or a strenuous day's working, although the exact cause is unknown. Ensuring the tail is dried thoroughly, especially at the base, after becoming wet will help prevent dead tail from occurring.

The tail is seen to hang limply from the base, or just below, and may be painful to touch. Rest is the main form of treatment with recovery usually seen within a week or so. Anti-inflammatory preparations may

urinary tract infection. There are different types of stone that need to be identified to ensure correct treatment. Although uncommon, Labradors have been noted to be susceptible to silica uroliths. If left untreated, they may have potentially life-threatening consequences by blocking the urethra and thereby preventing passage of urine. Stones can also form in the kidneys, causing severe abdominal pain while passing through the ureters.

- Renal failure: Kidneys can become damaged by infections, toxins or degenerate due to old age, resulting in reduced working capacity. Clinical signs are not obviously noticeable until more than three-quarters of the functioning tissue is affected. Early signs of kidney failure are drinking more and production of large volumes of dilute urine. As the disease progresses, vomiting, loss of appetite and lethargy are commonly noted.

- Tumours: Growths can occur in the bladder and cause problems by obstructing the flow of urine.

- Incontinence: This is an inability to control the act of urination and can have many contributing factors, such as infections, tumours and old age, affecting the ability of urine retention. Incontinence may be seen more commonly in the older, spayed female. Labradors have a higher incidence of incontinence relating to ectopic ureters (where the ureter opens into the urethra, vagina or uterus) than other breeds. It is often seen in young females, and surgery may be needed.

The cause of 'dead tail' is not known for sure, but it may be associated with swimming in cold water.

help with the pain and inflammation of the muscles. If there is no improvement then a visit to the vet is necessary, as there may be a further underlying cause of the limp tail, such as fracture or nerve damage.

INHERITED AND BREED-DISPOSED DISORDERS

The Labrador does have a few breed-related disorders, and if diagnosed with any of these diseases listed below, it is important to remember that they can affect offspring so breeding from affected dogs should be discouraged. The British Veterinary Association (BVA), the Kennel Club (KC) and the International Sheep Dog Society (ISDS) have set up various screening tests to enable breeders to check for affected individuals and hence reduce the prevalence of these diseases within the breed. There are also recognised DNA tests available to identify dogs with clear, carrier or affected status to specific diseases, the results being listed quarterly by the Kennel Club.

Elbow dysplasia (ED)

This is a developmental disease where the elbow does not mature correctly and signs of lameness are usually seen in younger, large-breed dogs. Labradors have a high incidence of ED, and the BVA/KC ED scheme is available to reduce the incidence within the breed. X-rays are taken by your veterinary surgeon and sent to the BVA where a panel will give a grading to each elbow. Surgery may be indicated to correct the abnormalities, and the affected joints will be more prone to arthritis later in life.

Hip dysplasia (HD)

This is where the ball-and-socket joint of the hip develops incorrectly so that the head of the femur (ball) and the acetabulum of the pelvis (socket) do not fit snugly. This causes pain in the joint and may be seen as lameness in dogs as young as five months old with deterioration into severe arthritis over time. Labradors are prone to HD and the BVA/KC HD scheme available involves a veterinary surgeon taking X-rays and sending them to the BVA

where a hip score, ranging from a possible perfect 0 to a deformed 106 total, is allocated determining the severity of disease. Careful and responsible breeding over the years has reduced the prevalence of this disease in Labradors, but care must be taken to ensure that this continues into the future.

Exercise-induced collapse

There is an inherited condition in Labradors where occasional exercise intolerance and collapse may be seen with strenuous exercise. Initial clinical signs may be seen in otherwise fit and healthy, generally over-excitable dogs between five months and five years. There is no definitive treatment and it is not usually fatal unless the dog is over-exercised. Affected individuals, identified by a DNA test, should not be bred from.

Retinal dysplasia

When the retina develops incorrectly, this may cause impaired vision and blindness depending on the degree of dysplasia and even detachment of the retina from the back of the eye. There are several forms of the disease that Labradors suffer from, varying in severity. The BVA/KC/ISDS eye scheme involves an eye examination to determine whether the dog is affected.

Generalised progressive retinal atrophy (GPRA)

GPRA is a bilateral degenerative disease of the cells (rods and cones) of the retina, leading initially to night blindness and progressing to complete loss of vision. Dogs are affected from three to four years of age and there is no cure. There is a prcd-GPRA DNA test available for younger dogs, before being used for breeding, to prevent carrier individuals passing on the genetic defect. Examination of the eyes under the BVA/CK/ISDS eye scheme identifies individuals once affected.

Hereditary cataracts

Cataracts are an opacification of the lens that tends to occur in older dogs. Labradors suffer from hereditary cataracts where the lens is often affected in younger dogs but may be seen later in life.

There are varying degrees of severity, the inherited form often having little effect on eyesight but, if necessary, surgery is usually successful to treat. The BVA/KC/ISDS eye scheme is available to detect, and prevent breeding from, affected individuals.

We are fortunate that the Labrador is a breed with no exaggeration and suffers from few inherited disorders.

Pets Passport

Dog owners now can take their furry friend with them when going abroad to certain countries, but this is not without rules and regulations. Your dog will have to have their own passport, issued and signed by a veterinary surgeon, for which he has to fill several criteria:

- Microchip
- Rabies vaccination
- Rabies blood test declaring suitable immunity against rabies (must be 21 days after vaccination and there must be six months between the blood test and returning to the UK)
- Tick and tapeworm treatment applied by a veterinary surgeon not less than 24 hours and not more than 48 hours before returning to the UK.

There are several canine diseases abroad that are not usually seen in the UK:

- Rabies: Caused by the rabies virus and only able to infect mammals. Rabies is present throughout the majority of Europe. Transmission is from the saliva of infected animals inoculated by a bite. The disease can be divided into the 'furious' and the 'dumb' forms. With the dumb form, the dog is seen to be almost paralysed, drooling and lethargic; the furious form is where the dog is a 'typical' rabid animal with an irrational urge to attack and bite. Both forms are infectious and will progress to paralysis and death. There is no treatment and vaccination is the only form of prevention.

- *Leishmania* species. These are intracellular parasites transmitted by sand flies, causing fever, lethargy, weight loss, skin scales, hair loss, anaemia, anorexia and shifting lameness. It can take months or even years for signs to show after infection has occurred. Care must be taken, as this disease is transmissible to humans via the sand fly from infected dogs. Treatment regimes are available and differ according to the particular species present, although there is no cure at this time.

- *Ehrlichia canis.* This is a parasite, transmitted by ticks, which reproduces inside white blood cells, causing a leucopaenia (low white-cell count), thrombocytopaenia (low platelet count) and fever. Death may occur due to secondary infections from low white blood cells or haemorrhages from low platelets (needed for clotting). Antibiotics are indicated for treatment.

- *Babesia canis.* This is a parasite transmitted by ticks, which reproduces inside the red blood cells and causes anaemia (low red cell count) and haemoglobinuria ('redwater'). Clinical signs are usually fever, anaemia, jaundice and haemoglobinuria, but, with acute cases, collapse and sudden death may occur. This is primarily a disease found in mainland Europe, Africa, Asia and the Americas. Prevention is by avoiding tick bites with a suitable acaricide before and during time abroad and removing any ticks as soon as possible.

The introduction of passports for dogs mean many more owners are able to take their dogs on holiday.

- *Dirofilaria immitis.* This is a 20- to 30-cm-long worm that is found in the right side of the heart and adjacent blood vessels. The females release microfilariae into the bloodstream, which are ingested by mosquitoes and transmitted to the next dog. This parasite is normally seen in warm climates. Clinical signs include coughing, weight loss, lethargy, respiratory problems, and, in severe cases, sudden death. Prevention is better than treatment and any dog travelling abroad should be treated regularly while away. If infection occurs, treatment is done with care, as toxic reactions can occur due to large numbers of dying worms and embolism.

SUMMING UP

It may give the pet owner cause for concern to find about health problems that may affect their dog. But it is important to bear in mind that acquiring some basic knowledge is an asset, as it will allow you to spot signs of trouble at an early stage. Early diagnosis is very often the means to the most effective treatment.

Fortunately, the Labrador is a generally healthy and disease-free dog with his only visits to the vet being annual check-ups. In most cases, owners can look forward to enjoying many happy years with this loyal companion.

With good care and management, your Labrador should live a long life and suffer few health problems.

Useful Addresses

BREED CLUBS
Please contact the Kennel Club to obtain contact information about breed clubs in your area.

KENNEL CLUBS
The Kennel Club (UK)
1 Clarges Street London, W1J 8AB
Telephone: 0870 606 6750
Fax: 0207 518 1058
Web: www.thekennelclub.org.uk

American Kennel Club (AKC)
5580 Centerview Drive, Raleigh, NC 27606.
Telephone: 919 233 9767
Fax: 919 233 3627
Email: info@akc.org
Web: www.akc.org

TRAINING AND BEHAVIOUR
Association of Pet Dog Trainers (APDT)
PO Box 17, Kempsford, GL7 4WZ
Telephone: 01285 810811
Email: APDToffice@aol.com
Web: http://www.apdt.co.uk

Association of Pet Behaviour Counsellors (APBC)
PO BOX 46, Worcester, WR8 9YS
Telephone: 01386 751151
Fax: 01386 750743
Email: info@apbc.org.uk
Web: http://www.apbc.org.uk/

ACTIVITIES
Agility Club
http://www.agilityclub.co.uk/

British Flyball Association
PO Box 990, Doncaster, DN1 9FY
Telephone: 01628 829623
Email: secretary@flyball.org.uk
Web: http://www.flyball.org.uk/

World Canine Freestyle Organisation
P.O. Box 350122, Brooklyn, NY 11235-2525
Telephone: 718 332-8336
Fax: 718 646-2686
Email: wcfodogs@aol.com
Web: www.worldcaninefreestyle.org

HEALTH
Alternative Veterinary Medicine Centre
Chinham House, Stanford in the Vale, Oxfordshire, SN7 8NQ
Telephone: 01367 710324
Fax: 01367 718243
Web: www.alternativevet.org/

Animal Health Trust
Lanwades Park, Kentford, Newmarket, Suffolk, CB8 7UU
Telephone: 01638 751000
Website: www.aht.org.uk

British Association of Veterinary Ophthalmologists (BAVO)
Email: secretary@bravo.org.uk
Web: http://www.bravo.org.uk/

British Small Animal Veterinary Association (BSAVA)
Woodrow House, 1 Telford Way, Waterwells Business Park, Quedgeley, Gloucestershire, GL2 2AB
Telephone: 01452 726700
Fax: 01452 726701
Email: customerservices@bsava.com
Web: http://www.bsava.com/

British Veterinary Hospitals Association (BHVA)
Station Bungalow, Main Rd, Stocksfield, Northumberland, NE43 7HJ
Telephone: 07966 901619
Fax: 07813 915954
Email: office@bvha.org.uk
Web: http://www.bvha.org.uk/

Royal College of Veterinary Surgeons (RCVS)
Belgravia House, 62-64 Horseferry Road, London, SW1P 2AF
Telephone: 0207 222 2001
Fax: 0207 222 2004
Email: admin@rcvs.org.uk
Web: www.rcvs.org.uk

ASSISTANCE DOGS
Canine Partners
Mill Lane, Heyshott, Midhurst, West Sussex, GU29 0ED
Telephone: 08456 580480
Fax: 08456 580481
www.caninepartners.co.uk

Dogs for the Disabled
The Frances Hay Centre, Blacklocks Hill, Banbury, Oxon, OX17 2BS
Telephone: 01295 252600
Web: www.dogsforthedisabled.org

Guide Dogs for the Blind Association
Burghfield Common, Reading, Berkshire, RG7 3YG
Telephone: 01189 835555
Fax: 01189 835433
Web: www.guidedogs.org.uk/

Hearing Dogs for Deaf People
The Grange, Wycombe Road, Saunderton, Princes Risborough,
Bucks, HP27 9NS
Telephone: 01844 348100
Fax: 01844 348101
Web: hearingdogs.org.uk

Pets as Therapy
3a Grange Farm Cottages, Wycombe Road, Saunderton, Princes Risborough, Bucks, HP27 9NS
Telephone: 01845 345445
Fax: 01845 550236
Web: http://www.petsastherapy.org/

Support Dogs
21 Jessops Riverside, Brightside Lane, Sheffield, S9 2RX
Tel: 01142 617800
Fax: 01142 617555
Email: supportdogs@btconnect.com
Web: www.support-dogs.org.uk

About The Authors

ANN M. BRITTON (BOWSTONES)
Ann was born into a well-known dog-showing family; the fourth generation descended from Victorian forebears whose lady pioneers re-launched the Ladies Kennel Association in 1904. The Bowstones prefix was registered with the Kennel Club in 1946 by her mother, a Toy and Utility judge, who also bred gundogs and Champion Cavalier King Charles and Shih Tzus. Ann attended her first dog show, Crufts, in 1948 and has been involved with showing and breeding dogs, and organising Championship dog shows most of her life.

Ann, an international Labrador judge, breeds and shows Labradors and owns four homebred Champions plus other top winners. She has been the weekly Labrador columnist for Our Dogs magazine for the past nine years, reviews books and writes articles for Labrador periodicals and general dog magazines both at home and abroad.

ESTELA BADEN BSc Hons BVSc MRCVS
Estela graduated as a veterinary surgeon from Liverpool University in 2006. Since qualifying she has been working in a small animal practice in Monmouthshire. Whilst interested in all aspects of small animal practice, she has particular interests in small animal surgery and animal behaviour.
See Chapter Six: Health Care for Labradors.

Further Reading

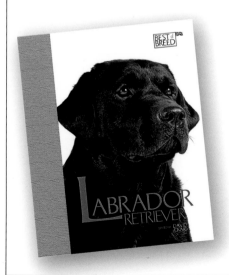

Labrador Retriever
(BEST OF BREED)

Written by leading British experts, including David Craig, *The Labrador Retriever* offers readers an unrivalled depth of knowledge about their chosen breed. The book gives detailed information on character and behaviour, puppy care, training and socialisation, with a special chapter on Labrador health written by a leading British vet. Illustrated by a stunning collection of more than 120 specially-commissioned colour photographs, matched by the high-specification production, and distinctively finished with real cloth binding, this is one breed book no Labrador lover should be without.

Available in the UK from Corpus Publishing, PO Box 8, Lydney, Gloucestershire, GL15 6YD. Tel: 01594 560600   Price: £14.99 (plus £2 p+p)

Index

Dogs for the Disabled
puppy
sponsor

Help us turn paws into helping hands

Sponsor a **Dogs for the Disabled** puppy for just £5.00 per month and you could help change someone's life.

www.dogsforthedisabled.org   **Telephone: 01295 252600**

Dogs for the
Disabled
Registered charity number: 1092960